The Gospel Story of Jesus

Jan Thompson

Edward Arnold
A division of Hodder & Stoughton
LONDON   MELBOURNE   AUCKLAND

To Christine, Jane and Barbara,
my R.E. colleagues at Bullers
Wood School, Chislehurst

Illustrated by Martin Pitts

© 1986 Jan Thompson
First published in Great Britain 1986
Second impression 1988

British Library Cataloguing in Publication Data

Thompson, Jan
    The Gospel story of Jesus.
    1. Jesus Christ
    I. Title
    232   BT301.2
    ISBN 0-7131-7592-3

All rights reserved. No part of this publication may be
reproduced or transmitted in any form or by any means,
electronically or mechanically, including photocopying,
recording or any information storage or retrieval system,
without either the prior permission in writing from the
publisher or a licence permitting restricted copying. In the
United Kingdom such licences are issued by the Copyright
Licensing Agency, 33–34 Alfred Place, London WC1E 7DP.

Acknowledgements

The Publishers would like to thank the following for their
permission to include copyright material: The American Bible
Society for scripture quotations from the Good News Bible,
© American Bible Society 1966, 1971, 1976, published by
the Bible Societies and Collins, used by permission; Darton,
Longman and Todd Limited, for an extract from Carlo Carretto:
Letters from the Desert published and copyright 1972 by
Darton, Longman and Todd, London and used by permission;
The General Synod of the Church of England for extracts from
the Nicene Creed which are © International Consultation on
English Texts and the extract from the Eucharistic Prayer in
the Order for Holy Communion Rite A in the Alternative
Service Book 1980 which is © Central Board of Finance of the
Church of England and reproduced by permission; Hodder &
Stoughton Limited for an extract from David Watson: *Fear no
Evil*; Oxford University Press for an illustration from S.H.
Hooke: *In the Beginning* (1979); Stainer and Bell Ltd for verses
from Sydney Carter: *When I Needed a Neighbour*; Superstar
Ventures Ltd for lyrics from Tim Rice and Andrew Lloyd
Webber: *Jesus Christ Superstar* reproduced by kind permission
of Superstar Ventures Ltd, copyright MCA Music Ltd and
Josef Weinberger Limited for verses from Patrick Appleford:
Living Lord copyright 1960 Josef Weinberger Ltd, reproduced
by permission of the copyright owners.

The Publishers would also like to thank the following for their
permission to reproduce copyright illustrations: Barnabys
Picture Library: pp 7 (H. Kauus), 36 (Tony Boxall), 42, 47
(Jonathan Rutland); Jan Thompson: pp 8, 14, 15, 44, 54, 67, 81;
Ronald Grant Archive: p 10; The British Society for the Turin
Shroud: p 11; Keith Ellis Collection: p 12; Coventry Cathedral:
p 16; British Library: pp 17, 18; Sonia Halliday: pp 21, 69;
BIPAC: pp 22, 57, 66, 68, 71; Church Missionary Society: p 23;
Biblioteca Nazionale Marciana, Venezia: p 26; The Tate
Gallery: p 28; A. F. Kersting: p 30; Derek G. Widdicombe: p 32;
United Society for the Propagation of the Gospel: p 37; Ryszard
Petrajtis/Muzeum Nardowe, Gdansk: p 39 l and r; The Mansell
Collection Ltd: pp 45, 84; St Marylebone Centre for Healing and
Counselling: p 48; Zefa: pp 50, 72; Lepra: p 53; Topham Picture
Library: p 56; Church Missionary Society: pp 59, 86; Merilyn
Thorold: pp 61 l, 78; Camera Press: pp 61 r, 79; Juliette Soester:
pp 63, 82; The Salvation Army: p 65; M. L. Taylor: p 76; Carlos
Reyes: p 85; Geoffrey Chapman: p 88; Jean-Luc Ray: p 89; Tish
Murtha: p 91; Wycliffe Bible Translators: pp 92, 93 l and r.

Printed in Great Britain for Edward Arnold, the educational,
academic and medical publishing division of Hodder and
Stoughton Limited, Mill Road, Dunton Green, Sevenoaks, Kent
by St Edmundsbury Press Limited, Bury St Edmunds, Suffolk.

Contents

To the teacher

The Gospel Story of Jesus is written mainly for pupils in the second and third years of secondary school; although it should also provide a useful introduction to some of the GCSE courses in Religious Studies and background material for them.

Its purpose is to explore the real nature of the Gospels: to ask what they are trying to tell us about Jesus; rather than to attempt to reconstruct a picture of the historical Jesus, which is fraught with difficulties.

So this book does *not* work chronologically through the life of Jesus but studies important themes, which give the book its seven main parts. It begins, not with the birth, but with the death and resurrection of Jesus. There is a theological reason for this, since without the Resurrection there would have been no Good News to tell. C. H. Dodd (in *The Apostolic Preaching and its Developments*) has argued that this was the core of the gospel proclaimed by the early Christians; and when they looked back over Jesus' ministry they interpreted everything in the light of the Cross and Resurrection. Therefore, when this book looks at Jesus' baptism and transfiguration, at his teaching, his miracles, the conflicts that he faced and at the birth narratives, it is asking throughout, 'What are the Gospel writers saying here about the meaning of Jesus?' And, finally, Part 7 shows that the Good News still has meaning for Christians today.

The Christmas stories are deliberately placed towards the end of the book. This is because they are likely to be the latest material in the Gospels and also because pupils will then be less inclined to assume that the Gospel story is a *biography* of Jesus. Also, they are dealt with at quite a difficult level, and it is advisable that pupils should be familiar with the book's approach before tackling this part.

It is necessary for pupils to take this theological approach to the Gospels if they study them at GCSE and beyond; and it is important that books used in the earlier stages of secondary education should lay the founda-

tions for this way of understanding them.

The basic content of this book is presented in short narratives, followed by 'Over to you' sections. Some of the questions here are designed to check that pupils have grasped the main points, and many of these could be answered orally in class. Others encourage pupils to read and understand parts of the Gospels for themselves, and these exercises will add more detail to the narrative in the book. Obviously, teachers should use the questions selectively.

At the end of the first six parts of the book I have suggested that pupils make illustrations on pieces of paper. These can be done in a variety of imaginative ways and then mounted in the form of a collage. As each section is added, a wall-mural can be built up of the Gospel story of Jesus.

You will notice boxed sections throughout the book. These provide more detailed background information and stimulus material for wider-ranging study. In general these sections are more difficult than the rest of the book. They have been kept separate so that the book can easily be used without referring to them if time is short, or if it is being used with less academic pupils.

A pack of *Gospel Resource Sheets* is available to complement this text-book; it consists of blackline masters of worksheets and information sheets. They develop the themes of this book by providing more work on some of the stories and topics already included here, by giving other stories and information to fill out the pupils' background knowledge and by introducing further parables and miracles of Jesus. They have been designed with homework particularly in mind so that all the information needed to answer the questions is provided, e.g. biblical quotations are printed out in full rather than just giving references.

It is difficult to know which is the best version of the Bible to use for they all have their advantages and drawbacks. The popular *Good News Bible* seems most suitable for lower to middle secondary school level and therefore it is used for the quotations in this book and on the Resource Sheets (except in a few instances, where stated, to retain some important imagery). This book can also be used with other versions of the Bible as long as the teacher is prepared to comment on any differences in the wording which could cause problems. This in itself is a valid educational exercise since pupils ought to be made aware that all English versions are translations from the original Hebrew or Greek.

My hope is that fellow teachers will find this material useful and that pupils will find it attractive, interesting and thought-provoking.

To the pupil

The Gospels — the first four books of the New Testament — provide us with nearly all the early information that exists about Jesus' life. Yet they are not biographies (life stories). Only two of the Gospels include birth stories, there is only one story of Jesus' childhood and there are no indications of what he looked like. They concentrate instead on the religious ministry of Jesus: the last few years of his life which he spent travelling around Palestine preaching to people about God and healing the sick. There is a particular emphasis on the stories which are connected with his death. The Gospels do not set out to prove that Jesus was a real historical person. That was not necessary, for they were written when many people still remembered Jesus.

The word *gospel* means 'good news' and the Gospel books were written by people who regarded Jesus as good news for the world. They were Christians — people who called Jesus the *Christ*, or *Messiah*. They believed in him as their Lord and Saviour; the only one who could rule over their lives and bring them close to God, not only in this world but in the life after death. They wanted to share this good news with others. After a time of preaching to anyone who would listen, they set about writing it down in the Gospels, so that the message would spread even further. John's Gospel makes this quite clear:

> But these have been written in order that you may believe that Jesus is the Messiah, the Son of God, and that through your faith in him you may have life. (John 20:31)

The Gospel Story of Jesus is not, therefore, an attempt to tell the story of Jesus' life, or to say what Jesus was like as a person. These things we shall probably never know for certain. Rather, it gives you a selection of stories from the Gospels to study under six themes, and asks why the Gospel writers included them and what they were trying to tell us about Jesus. You may not agree with their beliefs about Jesus. This book does not set out to convince you one way or the other. Its purpose is to give you some understanding of the picture of Jesus which is presented in the Gospels, and of the importance of Jesus for Christians.

5

GALILEE and PERAEA were ruled by Herod Antipas, a son of Herod the Great, from 4 BC to AD 39. It was in this northern region that Jesus grew up, in the town of *Nazareth*. Fishermen from the *Sea of Galilee* became some of his disciples, as well as Mary of *Magdala*. *Capernaum* on the shores of the Sea of Galilee became the headquarters of his mission in the north. He raised a widow's son to life at *Nain*.

ITURAEA and TRACHONITIS were ruled by Herod Philip, another son of Herod the Great, from 4 BC to AD 34.

JUDAEA and SAMARIA were ruled by Roman governors from AD 6 to 39. This was the most important area: the capital city of *Jerusalem* was there, established as the Jewish capital by King David about a thousand years before. Jesus died in Jerusalem. Another 'city of David' was *Bethlehem*, where David was born and where Jesus came across the blind man, Bartimaeus, and the tax-man, Zacchaeus. *Bethany* was where Jesus' friends Mary, Martha and Lazarus lived, and *Bethphage*, nearby, was probably where Jesus began his descent to Jerusalem for the last time, on an ass. *Emmaus* was where some of his disciples lived, whom Jesus appeared to after his resurrection.

The death of Jesus

Two people were walking the 12 km journey back to Emmaus. They had left the busy city of Jerusalem behind, to the east of them. They were among many other Jewish pilgrims who were pouring out of the Holy City, returning home after the Passover festival.

One of these two travellers was a man called Cleopas. We do not know who his companion was — maybe it was his wife. It was a spring day, the best time of year for such a walk. The hills were green from the winter's rain and flecked with the bright colours of spring flowers. Although everything around them was bursting into life, these two people looked thoroughly miserable. They were downcast and depressed, and talked of death.

They did not notice another traveller approach them. When he saw their gloomy faces he asked what was the matter. Cleopas asked him if he were the only person staying in Jerusalem who did not know what had happened there in the last few days. The stranger encouraged them to go on, so they explained:

'The things that happened to Jesus of Nazareth ... This man was a prophet and was considered by God and by all the people to be powerful in everything he said and did. Our chief priests and rulers handed him over to be sentenced to death, and he was crucified.'

They added:

'And we had hoped that he would be the one who was going to set Israel free!' (Luke 24:19—21)

So this was why they were in such low spirits. They had believed in this Jesus. They had been his followers, his disciples. They had thought that he was the saviour (called the Messiah) whom God had promised to send to the Jews. Now Jesus was dead and their hopes were dashed. They had obviously been mistaken. They had given up, packed their bags and were going home.

What about Jesus' other disciples, especially the little band that had always been with him known as the Twelve? One of these, Judas Iscariot, had actually betrayed Jesus to the

Today, the followers of Jesus still remember his suffering and death. Christian pilgrims visit the places in Jerusalem which commemorate the final events of his life. Here they are walking along the Via Dolorosa (The Way of Sorrows) — the road Jesus probably took to the place of crucifixion. Why do you think some groups of Christians carry a large wooden cross along this route?

7

'They took Jesus to a place called Golgotha, which means "The Place of the Skull"... Then they crucified him.' (Mark 15:22, 24) This hill stands outside the old city walls of Jerusalem. Why do you think some people believe this is where Jesus was crucified? This is one of a number of possible sites.

authorities. On the Thursday night he had led them to where Jesus was praying in the Garden of Gethsemane, just outside the city, on the Mount of Olives. He had pointed out Jesus to them by greeting him in the customary way, with a kiss. Later in remorse Judas hanged himself.

When Jesus was arrested, most of his disciples had run away under cover of darkness, fearing for their own safety; but Simon Peter had been brave enough to see where Jesus was taken. He followed him to the High Priest's house and waited in the courtyard. Jesus had given Simon the nickname Peter, which meant 'rock', for he was the strong one of the Twelve. Yet even Peter let Jesus down at the end. As he waited in the courtyard, sitting with other people around the fire, he was accused on three different occasions of being one of Jesus' followers. Each time Peter denied it more strongly. By this time dawn was breaking and Peter was suddenly overcome by guilt. It was the sound of a cock crowing that had reminded him of Jesus' prediction that he would fail him. Peter broke down and cried.

The eleven disciples were still in Jerusalem three days later, unsure what to do next. They were still in a state of shock for it had all happened so suddenly. On Thursday night Jesus had been arrested, and less than twenty-four hours later he was dead and buried. He had been convicted of religious crimes by the Jewish court under the High Priest. Then he was taken to Pilate, the Roman governor, who was persuaded to pass the death sentence on him. The disciples could hardly bear to think of Jesus' suffering. He had been mocked and humiliated, whipped and beaten, forced to carry the heavy wooden beam as far as he could to his place of execution, and finally nailed to it and left to die an agonising death on a cross.

For two or three years these eleven men had been Jesus' team, travelling around Palestine with him. Now the cross on which their leader had died stood on a hill just outside the city walls. It was a painful reminder that their movement, which had begun so hopefully, had now ended in public disgrace.

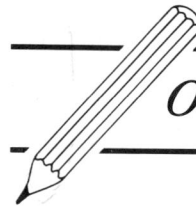

Over to you

1. Draw a picture of Cleopas and his companion on the road to Emmaus, trying to show how they were feeling.
2. Read the story of Peter's denials in Mark 14:66—72 or another Gospel.
   a) How do you think people knew that Peter was a northerner, from Galilee?
   b) What had Jesus prophesied about the cock crowing?
   c) Think of a time when you let someone down. How did you feel about it?
3. Read for yourself the story of Jesus' death in Mark 15:16—39 or another Gospel.
   a) Make a brief list of the events in the order in which they appear.
   b) What was done to Jesus to mock him as if he were a king? (Draw this if you prefer.) What title was put on the cross?
   c) Why would it seem fitting to the followers of Jesus that there should be darkness while Jesus was dying?
4. Look up Deuteronomy 21:22—3 and explain why Jews would regard Jesus' death as shameful.

A The curtain of the Temple

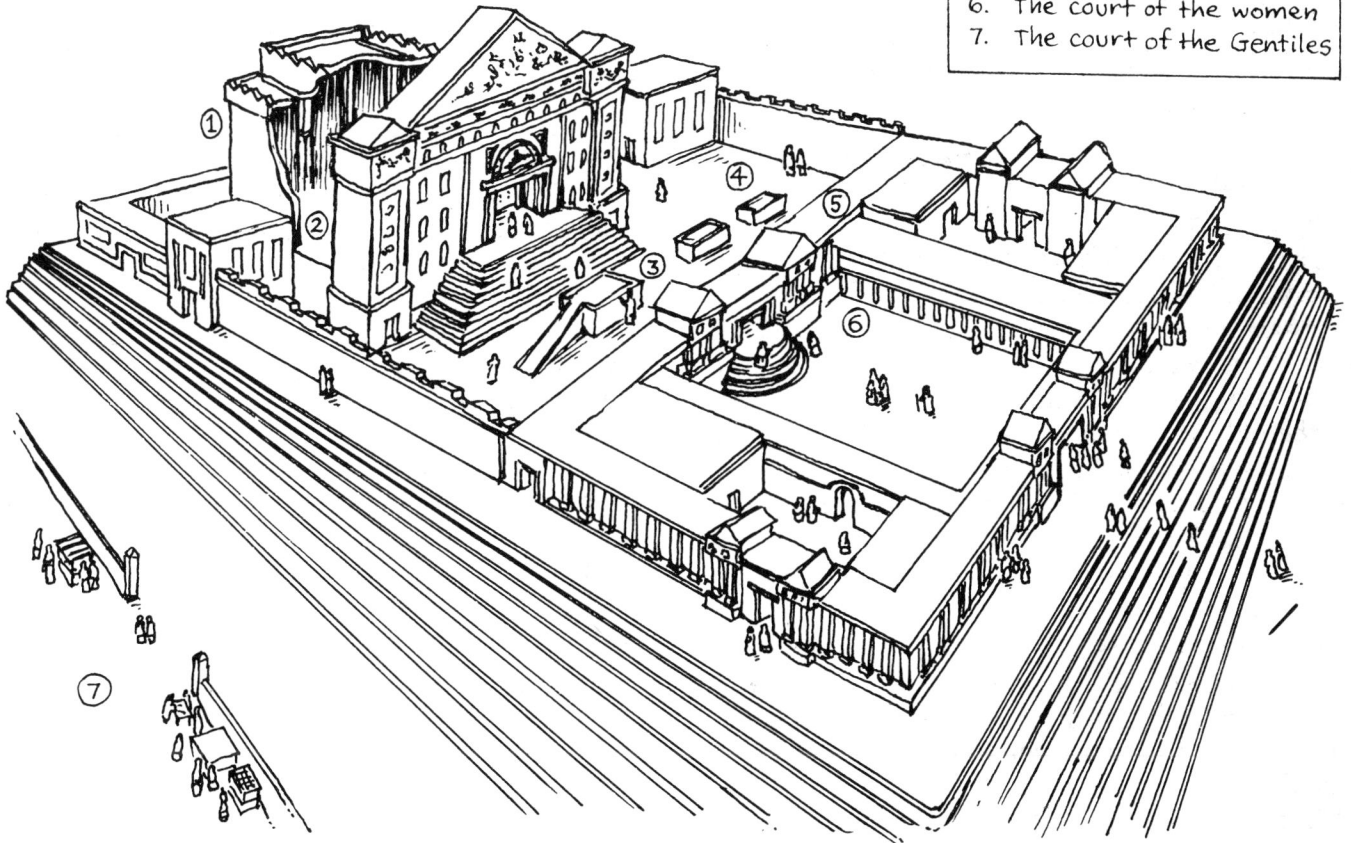

1. The Holy of Holies
2. The Holy Place
3. The altar
4. The court of the priests
5. The court for male Jews
6. The court of the women
7. The court of the Gentiles

A plan of the Temple in Jesus' day. The much bigger Court of Gentiles surrounded this on all sides.

The Gospels speak of the curtain of the Temple being torn apart at Jesus' death. This is symbolic.

The curtain of the Temple separated off the most sacred shrine, called the Holy of Holies, from the Holy Place (see diagram). Only the High Priest could go beyond this curtain and then only once a year at the Day of Atonement. This is the day when Jews ask God to forgive all their sins from the past year.

The picture of the curtain being torn open at Jesus' death represents the Christian belief that Jesus broke down barriers and gave ordinary people free access to God, who would always be willing to forgive their sins.

The Temple stood in the Court of the Priests. The priests offered sacrifices on the altar outside. They entered the Temple up a flight of stairs and through a wide porch. They were allowed into the Holy Place, but only the High Priest could go beyond the curtain into the Holy of Holies. Ordinary people were kept away from the Temple building which was quite small and regarded as too holy for them to enter. They gathered outside in the courtyards allotted to them, the women separated from the men, and the Jews separated from the Gentiles.

B Crucifixion

This was the Roman method of execution for all except Roman citizens (who were killed in a much quicker way, by being beheaded with a sword). The victim for crucifixion was fixed to a wooden cross and left to die a slow, agonising death in full public view as a warning to others. It could take as long as a week to die in this way but, mercifully, most prisoners died much sooner because of their previous treatment. They were usually flogged beforehand with leather whips studded with metal which flayed their backs. They were then made to carry the heavy cross-bar to the place of execution where the upright beam was already securely in place. The prisoner's arms were tied to the cross-bar, sometimes with his hands nailed to it through the wrists, which could take the weight. Then the cross-bar was hoisted up and fixed in place into a notch in the upright beam. The prisoner's feet were tied or nailed down, with a small wooden bar either beneath the feet or the crotch, to support the weight of the body. Here, exposed to the heat of the day and the cold of the night, without food or water, in pain from the wounds of the nails and the flogging and the severe cramp caused by the strain on the arms, shoulders and chest, the victim had to keep heaving his body upwards in order to breathe. As he weakened, death came eventually from suffocation.

1. *Using this information and Mark 15:21, comment on what Simon of Cyrene was made to do.*
2. *Using this information and Mark 15:25 and 33–7, comment on the length of time it took Jesus to die.*
3. *Look up Mark 15:23 and 36, and explain what was done for the victims to try to dull the pain of crucifixion.*
4. *Look up Mark 15:24, and explain what happened to the prisoner's clothes.*

This is the crucifixion scene from a modern film called Jesus. *Notice where the nail is which holds up Jesus' arm. It is not in the palm of the hand, as used to be thought. We now know that this would simply tear away. The Roman soldier is nailing the title to the top of the cross. It is written in three languages. Look up Mark 15:26 to find out what it says.*

C The Turin Shroud

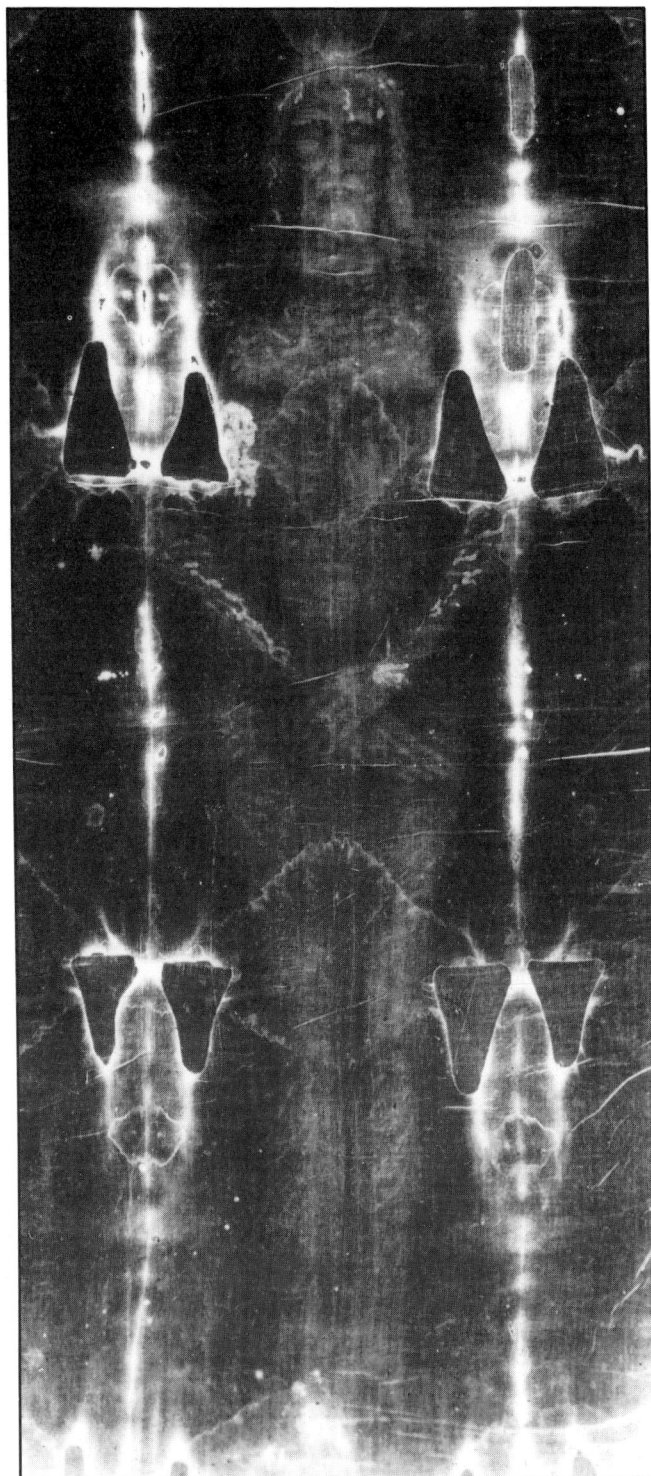

This photographic negative shows the half of the cloth which covered the front of the body. The outline of the body can be clearly seen if you ignore the four large marks caused by fire damage.

This is an ancient strip of linen cloth measuring 4.4 m long by 1.1 m wide. For the past 400 years it has been kept in Turin Cathedral in Italy because it is claimed to be the shroud in which Jesus' dead body was wrapped and laid in the tomb.

On this long strip of cloth there is the shadowy image of the front and back of a crucified man. It appears most clearly, as is shown here, in the negatives of black and white photographs that have been taken of it. The image is remarkable for its three-dimensional effect. When a hologram (a three-dimensional photograph) was made of the face, using the differences between dark and light on the cloth to represent a raising and lowering of the surface, it looked just like a relief model of a human face. This does not happen at all with an ordinary painting and suggests that the image was made on the cloth while it was wrapped around the face of a dead person.

The image is of a crucified man. There are blood flows from the head, marks of ninety to a hundred strokes on the back from a whip, marks of nails through the wrists and an extra blood flow from the side.

Scholars are divided over whether this is a genuine shroud, with the image made in some miraculous way, or just a clever hoax. Even if it were proved to have come from first-century Palestine there is no proof that it came from the body of Jesus. Even so, if it is genuine, it provides useful evidence of crucifixion at that time.

1. *Look up John 19:1–2 and 34. How do the details in these verses correspond with the evidence from the Turin Shroud?*

The Resurrection

The two disciples on the road to Emmaus had given up hope in Jesus, despite having heard rumours of his empty tomb and stories of angels (see section **D**). After all, who would believe such things? Then the stranger began to speak. He reminded them of passages in their Scriptures which showed them that God's way could require suffering. He explained that it was quite possible, after all, to believe in a crucified Messiah. He taught them to see Jesus' death as part of God's whole plan to save humanity and not as some dreadful mistake.

By this time they had reached their destination and they persuaded the stranger to stay with them. At the meal table the stranger took the bread, said grace over it and broke it, as was the Jewish custom. Suddenly, in this familiar action, the man was a stranger no longer, but Jesus himself. Then he disappeared. The two disciples were so excited that they immediately travelled all the way back to Jerusalem that night. They found the eleven disciples also overjoyed and declaring:

'The Lord is risen indeed! He has appeared to Simon!' (Luke 24:34)

A number of experiences like this are recorded of the disciples being made aware of the risen Jesus among them (see section **E**). These experiences explain how such dispirited people could change so dramatically. Their sorrow and despair turned to joy and hope once more, and the Cross became for them not a sign of failure but of victory over death. Both the stories of the empty tomb and those which tell of Jesus' resurrection appearances explain how the disciples came to cope with Jesus' death and to understand his crucifixion as a necessary part of his mission as the Messiah.

Not long afterwards the disciples came out of hiding and were heard preaching the gospel on the streets of Jerusalem. They were no longer afraid, for they were convinced that in some way Jesus would always be with them. This was the message that they preached (taken from one of Peter's sermons, as recorded in the Book of the Acts of the Apostles):

'Listen to these words, fellow-Israelites! Jesus of Nazareth was a man whose divine authority was clearly proven to you by all the miracles and wonders which God performed through him. You yourselves know this, for it happened here among you. In accordance with his own plan God had already decided that Jesus would be handed over to you; and you killed him by letting sinful men crucify him. But God raised him from death, setting him free from its power, because it was impossible that death should hold him prisoner. .... All the people of Israel, then, are to know for sure that this Jesus, whom you crucified, is the one that God has made Lord and Messiah!' (Acts 2:22–4, 36)

The risen Jesus was recognised in the breaking of bread. Jesus had broken bread with his disciples just before his death, at the Last Supper. Look up Luke 22:19 to find out what Jesus said the bread stood for. This is re-enacted in churches today. In this picture, a Methodist minister is giving a small piece of bread to a believer to eat.

Over to you

1. Copy out Jesus' words from Luke 24:26 which explain that it was necessary for the Messiah to suffer.
2. Followers of Christ are called Christians. Today, some of them wear a cross on a chain round their necks. This is no longer a sign of death and disgrace, like a noose would be, but a symbol of life and victory. Where else might you find Christians using the symbol of the cross? List as many examples as possible.
3. a) What are the two references made to Simon Peter, the leader of the disciples, in the section you have just read?
   b) Remembering what happened on the night of Jesus' arrest, why do you think Peter is given a special mention?
4. Who was said to have raised Jesus from death?
5. What did Jesus' resurrection prove to Christians about him? (See the end of Peter's sermon.)
6. Read one of the Gospel accounts of the women finding the empty tomb, from section **D**. When did the women go to the tomb? (The *Sabbath* was the Jewish holy day — a religious holiday when work was forbidden.)
7. Choose another resurrection appearance from the list in section **E**. Look it up and read it in the Bible.
   a) Record it in some way (e.g. write the story in your own words, perhaps imagining that you were one of the characters involved; or draw a picture of it).
   b) Why do you think the writer thought it was important to include this story in his Gospel? (i.e. What does it tell us about Jesus?)
8. Think about the words of this Christian chorus. Then explain where Christians today look for evidence of the Resurrection, apart from in the Bible:

He lives, he lives, Christ Jesus lives today.
He walks with me, he talks with me, along life's narrow way.
He lives, he lives, salvation to impart.
You ask me how I know he lives?
He lives within my heart!

D Finding the empty tomb

Time sequence of events

Thursday night: Jesus was arrested
Friday: Jesus was crucified and buried
Friday evening to Saturday night: The Sabbath day
Sunday morning: Jesus' empty tomb was discovered

Mark 16: 1–8

(The earliest known versions of Mark's Gospel end abruptly here.)

After the Sabbath was over, Mary Magdalene, Mary the mother of James, and Salome bought spices to go and anoint the body of Jesus. Very early on Sunday morning, at sunrise, they went to the tomb. On the way they said to one another, 'Who will roll away the stone for us from the entrance to the tomb?' (It was a very large stone.) Then they looked up and saw that the stone had already been rolled back. So they entered the tomb, where they saw a young man sitting on the right, wearing a white robe — and they were alarmed.

'Don't be alarmed,' he said, 'I know you are looking for Jesus of Nazareth, who was crucified. He is not here — he has been raised! Look, here is the place where they put him. Now go and give this message to his disciples, including Peter: "He is going to Galilee ahead of you; there you will see him, just as he told you."'

So they went out and ran from the tomb, distressed and terrified. They said nothing to anyone, because they were afraid.

Luke 23:55–24:11

The women who had followed Jesus from Galilee went with Joseph and saw the tomb and how Jesus' body was placed in it. Then they went back home and prepared the spices and perfumes for the body.

On the Sabbath they rested, as the Law commanded.

Very early on Sunday morning the women went to the tomb, carrying the spices they had prepared. They found the stone rolled away from the entrance to the tomb, so they went in; but they did not find the body of the Lord Jesus. They stood there puzzled about this, when suddenly two men in bright shining clothes stood by them. Full of fear, the women bowed down to the ground, as the men said to them, 'Why are you looking among the dead for one who is alive? He is not here; he has been raised. Remember what he said to you while he was in Galilee: "The Son of Man must be handed over to sinful men, be crucified, and three days later rise to life." '

Then the women remembered his words, returned from the tomb, and told all these things to the eleven disciples and all the rest. The women were Mary Magdalene, Joanna, and Mary the mother of James; they and the other women with them told these things to the apostles. But the apostles thought that what the women said was nonsense, and they did not believe them.

Matthew 28:1–10

After the Sabbath, as Sunday morning was dawning, Mary Magdalene and the other Mary went to look at the tomb. Suddenly there was a violent earthquake; an angel of the Lord came down from heaven, rolled the stone away, and sat on it. His appearance was like lightning, and his clothes were white as snow. The guards were so afraid that they trembled and became like dead men.

The angel spoke to the women. 'You must not be afraid,' he said. 'I know you are looking for Jesus, who was crucified. He is not here; he has been raised, just as he said. Come here and see the place where he was lying. Go quickly now, and tell his disciples, "He has been raised from death, and now he is going to Galilee ahead of you; there you will see him!" Remember what I have told you.'

So they left the tomb in a hurry, afraid and yet filled with joy, and ran to tell his disciples.

Suddenly Jesus met them and said, 'Peace be with you.' They came up to him, took hold of his feet, and worshipped him. 'Do not be afraid,' Jesus said to them. 'Go and tell my brothers to go to Galilee, and there they will see me.'

1. Make a note of how Luke's account is more miraculous than that of Mark.
2. What additional details are found in Matthew's account?
3. Which of these writers best puts across the earth-shattering nature of Jesus' resurrection, which he believed had brought into being a New World, a new age of salvation?

E Resurrection appearances

The earliest known copies of Mark's Gospel end abruptly at chapter 16 verse 8. We do not know if Mark originally recorded any resurrection appearances.

Matthew's Gospel

★ Jesus met Mary of Magdala and Mary the mother of James and Joseph as they hurried away from the empty tomb. He gave them a message for the eleven disciples. (28:8-10)
★ Jesus met his eleven disciples on a mountain in Galilee. He gave them authority to preach the gospel, and promised to be with them always. (28:16-20)

Luke's Gospel

★ Jesus walked with Cleopas and his companion on the road to Emmaus. They did not recognise him until he broke bread with them. (24:13-32)
★ It is simply recorded that Jesus had appeared to Simon Peter. (24:34)
★ Jesus appeared to the disciples in Jerusalem. He ate some fish to prove he was real. He took them out to Bethany, where he blessed them and then parted from them. (24:36-51)

John's Gospel

★ Jesus appeared to Mary of Magdala outside the empty tomb, and at first she mistook him for the gardener. (20:11-18)
★ Jesus appeared to the disciples, blessed them and gave them his power to continue his work. Thomas was absent on this occasion. (20:19-23)
★ A week later Jesus appeared again to the disciples, to convince Thomas that he had risen. (20:26-9)
★ Jesus appeared to the disciples by the Sea of Galilee (or Tiberias). (21:1-14) (In the rest of this chapter Jesus speaks especially to Simon Peter.)

The photograph on p. 14 shows a typical tomb in Palestine from the time of Jesus: a cave dug into the hillside. A round stone was rolled along a groove outside the entrance, to act as a door. You can just see the edge of it in the picture (marked by the arrow), since the tomb is open. The photograph on this page shows a similar stone, now displayed against a wall.

These pictures show a tomb which was discovered near to the hill shown in p. 8. It is now called the Garden Tomb and thought by some people to be the place where Jesus was buried. Notice the groove on the outside, along which the stone would have been rolled. Inside the tomb there is a ledge, now broken, on which a corpse would have been put.

This is part of the great tapestry in Coventry Cathedral, designed by Graham Sutherland. How can you tell that it is of the risen Jesus, after his crucifixion? (Clue: look at his hands.) Look at the expression on his face, and in his eyes. What is Jesus like in this picture?

The Gospels

The disciples preached the good news that Jesus was 'Lord and Messiah' and, following Jewish ideas, they believed that he would return in glory one day to judge the world. So it was important to spread the message about Jesus as quickly as possible, to as many people as possible, so that they could accept Jesus as their Lord and be saved on the Day of Judgment.

After about thirty years it became necessary not just to preach it but to write down this good news (or gospel) in books which were called *Gospels*. By this time the new religion of Christianity had taken root and Christian groups, called *churches*, were growing up all over the Roman world. These churches needed Christian Scriptures to study, to read in services and to teach from. Also, many of the first disciples were dying out, some of them becoming martyrs for their faith. So it became important to preserve the stories of the words and works of Jesus in writing, to record for all time the good news that Jesus was the Messiah.

There are four of these Gospels in the Christian Bible. They are called by the names of Matthew, Mark, Luke and John, who were thought to have written them. Each writer has presented his own picture of Jesus from the information he had available. Much of the information is the same in more than one Gospel, and sometimes the same material is found in all four Gospels. This is not surprising, for they were all about the same person; and it is probable that Mark's Gospel was known to Matthew and Luke. There are also differences between the Gospels, sometimes in the different stories they record and sometimes in the details of similar stories. This should not surprise us either. The stories were passed down by word of mouth over a period of thirty years or so and, however good their memories were, details do get changed in the telling.

Think of the Gospels like four people's projects on the person of Jesus. These writers gather their material together, getting some of it from the same places as each other, and finding some information that no one else has got. Once the first project is finished, the other writers may use parts of it, changing it slightly where they disagree with it or think they can improve upon it. They each have their own particular interests, which influence their choice of what they will include and what they will give most importance to. They have their own ways of organising the material into a particular order. So in the end there are four distinctive projects but they are all about the same person.

This shows the end of Luke's Gospel in the famous Codex Alexandrinus — a copy of the Bible from the early 5th century (called a codex because it is in book form). It is written in Greek capital letters without any gaps between the words. Greek was the language in which the Gospels were first written.

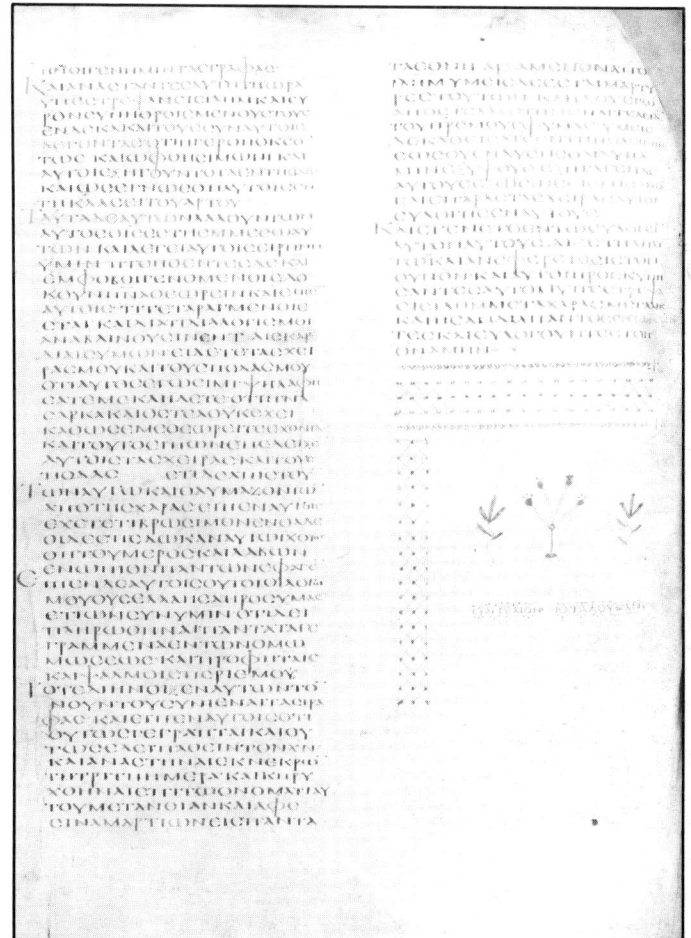

In the same way, the four Gospels give us four different writers' pictures of Jesus. But when all is said and done, they are all *Gospels* because they all present the *good news* that Jesus is the Saviour. Each writer has looked through the stories about Jesus with this in mind and has chosen those which seemed to put across most clearly 'the Good News about Jesus Christ, the Son of God'. (Mark 1:1)

This is the opening page of one of the four Gospels, written by monks on the Northumbrian island of Lindisfarne at the end of the 7th century. It is written in Latin, but the name of the Gospel is similar in English. Can you tell which it is? Notice the beautiful illuminated capital letter. Try to write your own name in this style. Latin took over from Greek as the main language.

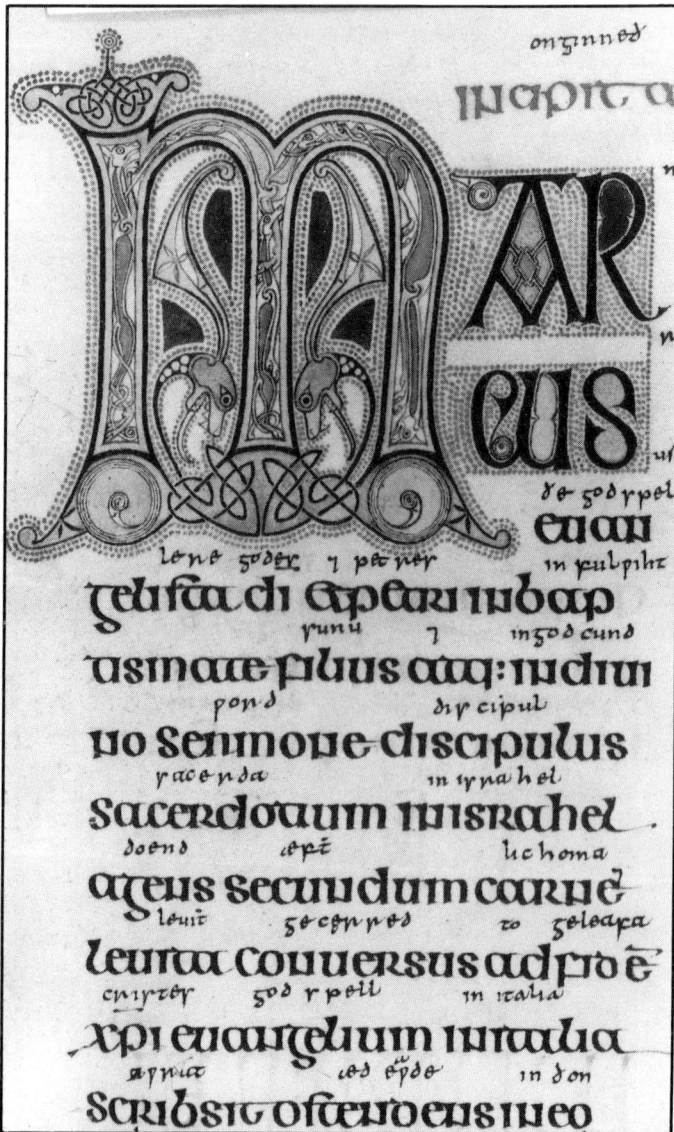

against me, how many times do I have to forgive him? Seven times?"

22 "No, not seven times," answered Jesus, "but seventy times seven,[r] 23 because the Kingdom of heaven is like this. Once there was a king who decided to check on his servants' accounts. 24 He had just begun to do so when one of them was brought in who owed him millions of pounds. 25 The servant did not have enough to pay his debt, so the king ordered him to be sold as a slave, with his wife and his children and all that he had, in order to pay the debt. 26 The servant fell on his knees before the king. 'Be patient with me,' he begged, 'and I will pay you everything!' 27 The king felt sorry for him, so he forgave him the debt and let him go.

28 "Then the man went out and met one of his fellow-servants who owed him a few pounds. He grabbed him and started choking him. 'Pay back what you owe me!' he said. 29 His fellow-servant fell down and begged him, 'Be patient with me, and I will pay you back!' 30 But he refused; instead, he had him thrown into jail until he should pay the debt. 31 When the other servants saw what had happened, they were very upset and went to the king and told him everything. 32 So he called the servant in. 'You worthless slave!' he said. 'I forgave you the whole amount you owed me, just because you asked me to. 33 You should have had mercy on your fellow-servant, just as I had mercy on you.' 34 The king was very angry, and he sent the servant to jail to

[r] seventy times seven; *or* seventy-seven times.
18.22: Gen 4.24

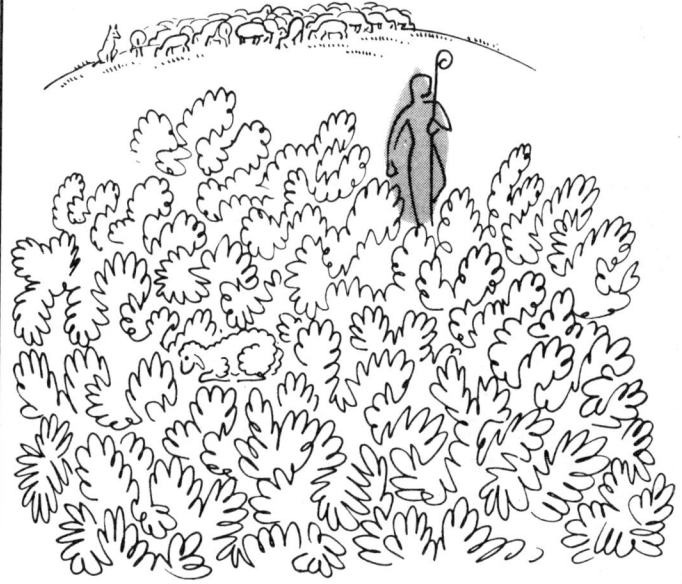

He will . . . go and look for the lost sheep (18.12)

This is a page from a modern English version of the Bible, known as the Good News Bible. *This is the version used in this book. Which Gospel is this page taken from?*

Over to you

1. What reason is given here for the fact that Christians at first thought it was important to preach the gospel, but not to write it down?
2. What other reasons might there have been for not writing the Gospels immediately?
3. Give two reasons why they eventually did write the Gospels.
4. What reason does John give in John 20:31?
5. What other reasons did Luke have when writing his Gospel? He explains these in Luke 1:1-4.

Art work

Look back over all you have done in Part 1. 'The Cross' means for Christians not just Jesus' suffering and death but also his victory as the Messiah. Try to convey this idea in some way in a picture for display.

Make sure you can spell
crucifixion (remember there is a cross in it)
resurrection (remember there is only one 's' as in the word 'rise')

Important words

Check the meaning of the following words by looking them up in the Word list at the back of this book. This is the order in which they occur in Part 1:

pilgrim	**resurrection**
disciple	**angel**
to crucify/crucifixion	**gospel**
Messiah	**martyr**
Christian/Christianity	

F *How the Gospels are related to each other*

Matthew, Mark and Luke are known as the *Synoptic Gospels*. The word *synoptic* can mean 'seen together' and 'similar view'. It describes the fact that these first three Gospels have such a lot in common that they can easily be compared with each other. John's Gospel, on the other hand, has many differences from the Synoptic Gospels, e.g. in its order of events, its characters, the type of material it includes and its outlook on several important religious topics.

This diagram shows the generally accepted theory as to how the Synoptic Gospels are related.

★ It is thought that Mark's Gospel was used by both Matthew and Luke when writing their Gospels. Only about 30 verses of Mark's Gospel contain material which is not found somewhere in Matthew and Luke; and over half of Mark's actual wording is reproduced in them.

★ Matthew and Luke must also have had a common source apart from Mark. They have about 200 similar verses which do not come from Mark's Gospel. We do not know what this source was, so it is simply called *Quelle* (or Q) which, in German, means 'Source'.

★ Matthew's Gospel also has material not found in any of the other Gospels (M); and so does Luke's Gospel (L).

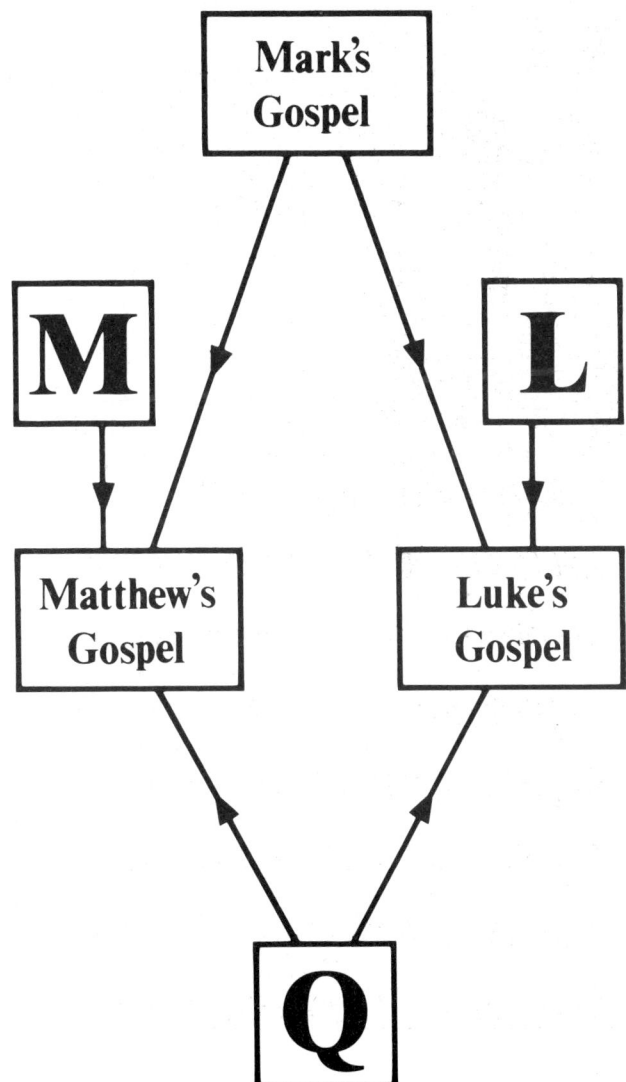

Mark's Gospel → Matthew's Gospel; Mark's Gospel → Luke's Gospel; M → Matthew's Gospel; L → Luke's Gospel; Q → Matthew's Gospel; Q → Luke's Gospel

John the Baptist

The Gospel story begins with a wild figure emerging from the desert and declaring that the end of the world is near. He is dressed in a rough coat, woven from camel hair and tied at the waist with a leather belt. He lives on locusts and wild honey.

The Jews of that time probably did not find John the Baptist such a strange and frightening sight as we should today. They had been brought up on stories of the great religious teachers of the past, called the prophets. One of these, the prophet Elijah, was described in their Scriptures as a hairy man who wore a leather belt. Elijah had lived nine hundred years earlier, but he was still an important figure in Judaism. Every year at the Passover supper, a special place was set at table for Elijah and the door was left ajar for him to come in (just as we might leave out a mince pie for Father Christmas!). This showed that the Jews expected Elijah to return one day. The prophet Malachi had foretold that he would come back to warn people of the Day of Judgment at the end of the world:

'But before the great and terrible day of the LORD comes, I will send you the prophet Elijah.' (Malachi 4:5)

Other prophecies spoke of one who would come to prepare the way for the Messiah:

The LORD Almighty answers, 'I will send my messenger to prepare the way for me. Then the Lord you are looking for will suddenly come to his Temple.' (Malachi 3:1)

A voice cries out,
'Prepare in the wilderness a road for the LORD!
Clear the way in the desert for our God!'
(Isaiah 40:3)

It seems that John the Baptist saw himself in this role: as a prophet (a spokesman for God), a 'voice' crying out and heralding the coming of the Messiah. Certainly this was how he appeared to the people of his day. He called them to repent of their sins so that they would be ready for the Messiah when he appeared and so be saved at the Day of Judgment. He took them down into the murky green waters of the river Jordan and baptized them there, washing their bodies with water as a symbol of their sins being washed away.

John the Baptist was preparing people to recognise and receive the Messiah when he came, the Jewish Saviour. He insisted that he was not himself the Messiah — he only poured water on people, but the Messiah would pour out upon them the Holy Spirit, bringing the power of God among them. The Jews were used to language like this; John the Baptist sounded just like their prophets of old:

'Afterwards I will pour out my spirit on everyone:
your sons and daughters will proclaim my message;
your old men will have dreams,
and your young men will see visions.'
(Joel 2:28)

Their prophets had lived hundreds of years ago, and since then God had been strangely silent. The prophets had delivered God's words to the people, but for the last five hundred years there had been no new revelations from God. The Jews longed for God to speak to them directly once more; and they believed that this would happen when God decided to send them the Messiah to save them. And now here was John the Baptist, speaking with the authority of a prophet and telling them that the day of salvation, for which they were all waiting, was near at hand. It was no wonder that crowds flocked to hear John, and many were baptized.

Over to you

Some Christians travel to the Holy Land especially to be baptized in the river Jordan, where Jesus was baptized. Pilgrims often bring back water from the Jordan, which may be used for baptisms back home.

1. Draw a picture of John the Baptist preaching. Try to show what you imagine him to have looked like.
2. Why was John given the title 'The Baptist'?
3. Of whom did John the Baptist remind people?
4. How do you imagine that John did his baptisms? Present your answer in a drawing or diagram if you wish.
5. Read the account of John's death in Mark 6: 17–29. Then copy out and complete the following sentences:
   a) John offended Herod Antipas, the Jewish ruler of Galilee, because he criticised him for _____
   b) Herod punished him by _____
   c) Herodias wanted John killed and her opportunity came when _____
   d) Herod promised to give Herodias' daughter anything she wanted and her mother persuaded her to ask for _____
   e) Herod agreed, even though he did not really want to kill John because _____
   f) After John's death, his disciples _____

21

A The Essenes

In Jesus' day there was an order of Jewish monks called the Essenes. Like some other Jewish groups they were destroyed when the Romans crushed the Great Revolt of the Jews of AD 66-70. We know about them from the writings of the Jewish historian, Josephus, who lived at that time, and also from the Dead Sea Scrolls. From 1947 these scrolls began to be found in a number of caves in the desert by the Dead Sea, and the remains of a Jewish monastery were uncovered nearby at Qumran. The scrolls were mostly copies of the Jewish Scriptures but some contained the rules, prayers and hymns of a monastic community. It is thought that Essene monks once lived there and that they hid their writings in the surrounding caves for safe keeping when the Romans attacked.

The Essenes were very strict monks and it was not easy to join them. They slept in caves or tents in the desert and lived and worked in the monastery during the day. The remains of a pottery have been found there,

Can you see the caves in the cliff face? It was in these and others like them that the Dead Sea Scrolls were found, written by the monks of Qumran.

and the writing room where the scrolls were copied out.

They applied the prophecy of Isaiah 40:3 to themselves (see p. 20), preparing themselves for the great battle which they believed would take place at the end of the world between the forces of good and evil. They called themselves the 'sons of light' and were certain that they would overcome the 'sons of darkness' and that their community would become the true Israel. They tried to keep themselves pure, awaiting the coming of their Messiahs (a priestly Messiah as well as the kingly one whom all Jews expected) to lead them in this final battle.

One of their rituals which symbolised their purity was that the monks bathed frequently in a pool, rather like a small swimming pool, with steps leading down into it. This can still be seen at Qumran today. Another religious ceremony which emphasised their brotherhood was the common meal that they shared in silence twice a day.

1. *It has been suggested that John the Baptist was a monk from Qumran. How many points can you make to support this theory?*
2. *Can you think of any arguments against this theory?*

B Baptism

In an open-air church service in Nigeria, a new-born baby is baptized. Its head is being splashed with water. What symbol of Christianity can you see in this picture?

Baptism is found in many religions. It is a religious ritual in which water is used, e.g. people bathe in it or have it sprinkled on their heads. Baptism has two basic symbolic meanings:

a Since water is used for washing, baptism is an outward symbol of inner purity — the cleansing of the soul from sin.

b Since water is essential for life, baptism is an outward symbol of inner, spiritual life.

In Judaism

Baptism was practised in Judaism. The Jewish Law laid down instructions for bathing in a special pool or bath of 'living' water (i.e. rain water or water from a running stream). Jews bathed in this pool to make themselves ritually clean, so that they could take part in religious services. Women during menstruation were considered 'unclean' as were people who had come in contact with a dead body or with someone else who was 'unclean', like a leprosy sufferer. They needed to be ritually cleansed. Many Jewish women still practise this seven days after the end of their period. In Israel today every Jewish bride must attend this ritual bath at the synagogue before she can be married. Ritual bathing was also introduced for people who converted to Judaism, before they were considered to be Jewish; and this is still done today.

In first-century Judaism, the Essene monks were known to practise frequent ritual washing, as they were especially concerned to keep themselves pure so that they would be saved at the Last Day.

The baptism offered by John the Baptist in the river Jordan was also to prepare people for the coming of the Messiah at the Day of Salvation, but we presume that people were only baptized by him once. It was a sign that they had turned their backs on their old, selfish ways and were making a new start in life. The washing was a sign that God had washed away their sins.

In Christianity

We know that Jesus was baptized by John the Baptist, but we do not know if Jesus baptized his own disciples. There are some hints in John's Gospel that he did, and certainly the Christian Church practised baptism soon after Jesus' death and still does so today. Christian baptism is done only once to a person. There are a variety of ways in which the different Churches now practise baptism, and it has a number of meanings:

a John the Baptist had said that he only baptized people with water but the Messiah would baptize them with the Holy Spirit — in other words, he would bring the power of God upon the people. The Church believes that the water of baptism is the outward sign that God the Holy Spirit comes inwardly to the believer.

b Early Christian baptism contained the idea of drowning your old self and rising to a new life in Christ. This idea is still evident in Churches where the person being baptized is completely submerged under the water for a moment. Some Churches prefer this: they believe it is closer to the baptism that John the Baptist practised and with which their Lord Jesus was baptized.

c Christian baptism also came to include the washing away of sins — particularly 'original sin', i.e. the basic selfishness in everyone, including babies. This makes sense of infant baptism, where the baby's head is sprinkled with water and then signed with the sign of the Cross.

d Baptism was also a sign that a person had become a member of the Church. This is why the font, which holds the water for baptism, is usually situated near the entrance to a church, just inside the building. Just as a person is born into a physical family, so they can be reborn into the spiritual family of Christianity.

You can see traditional stone fonts like this in many old churches. Fonts are used for the baptism of babies. They are shaped like a basin at the top, to hold the water.

1. *Look up John 3:22 and 4:1–2. What does this tell us about the use of baptism in Jesus' movement?*
2. *What meaning is given to John the Baptist's baptism in Mark 1:4?*
3. *Compare this to the teaching on Christian baptism in Acts 2:38.*
4. *Explain why baptism is a good symbol for repentance. (Look up 'repentance' in the Word list if necessary.)*
5. *What meaning is given to Christian baptism in Romans 6:4?*

Jesus' baptism

One of the many who responded to John's call to be baptized was Jesus himself. This is how Mark describes the importance of Jesus' baptism:

> As soon as Jesus came up out of the water, he saw heaven opening and the Spirit coming down on him like a dove. And a voice came from heaven, 'You are my own dear Son. I am pleased with you.' (Mark 1:10–11)

This short description is full of picture-language. It uses symbols to express the significance of this event. The Jews had prayed for God to 'tear the sky apart and come down' (Isaiah 64:1) and this passage shows us that he was thought to have done just that at Jesus' baptism. This was seen as the moment when the lines between God and his people were reconnected. God could speak to them once more because Jesus, the 'Son of God', the Messiah, had arrived.

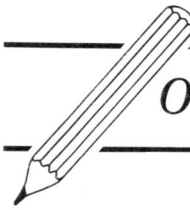

Over to you

1. This diagram shows how the Bible describes the universe. It speaks of God as if he lived up above the sky, in heaven. So what does the picture-language of 'heaven opening' mean? What is this saying about the access between God and humanity?

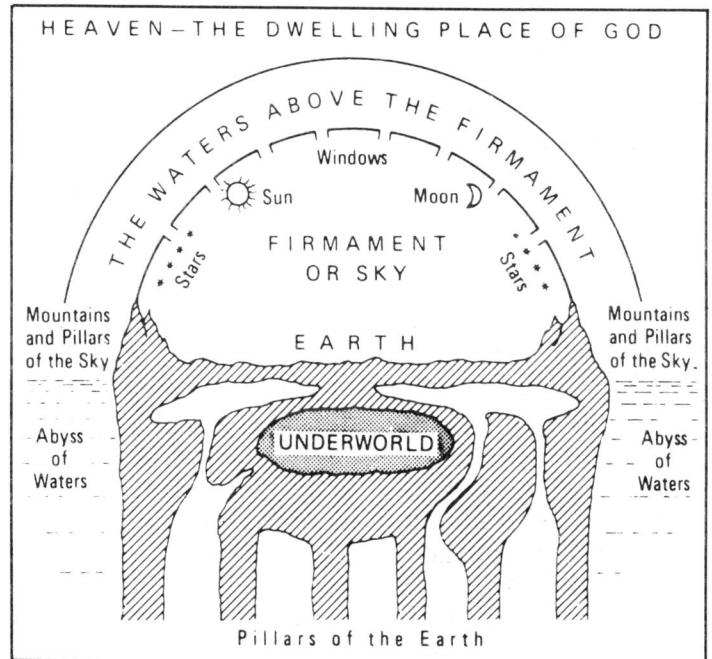

2. The *Spirit* refers to God as he works within people. Why do you think the image of a dove is used here to represent God's Spirit?
3. 'A voice came from heaven.' Whose voice do we assume is meant here?
4. What is Jesus called that meant that he was the Messiah?

C The Messiah

The Jews of first-century Palestine were keenly awaiting a saviour to be sent by God, whom they called the Messiah. They were expecting him to appear at any time. There had been leaders claiming to be the Messiah before Jesus, and there were more after him. The people were only too ready to follow these Messianic figures, for they believed that God must act soon to save them from their enemies.

The idea of the Messiah went right back to the time when the Jews had their own kingdom. Their kings were anointed with holy oil, and that is what 'Messiah' meant — 'the anointed one'. The title *Christ* was the Greek for 'anointed one' and therefore was another name for the Messiah in New Testament times.

Great King David in the Bible was anointed by the prophet Samuel. He was chosen out of all his brothers, even though he was the youngest. Jesus was anointed at his baptism by the prophet John. Christians believe he was the Messiah, the 'anointed one' — also known as the Son of David.

The greatest king of the Jews had been David who had ruled a great kingdom and empire around 1000 BC. The Jewish kingdom had gone out of existence in 600 BC, and for most of the time since then the Jews had been subject to one or other of the great world powers. In Jesus' day it was the Romans who ruled Palestine. During all that time, the Jews believed that God would one day free them from the hands of their enemies. The idea arose that God would send them another David, a new 'King of the Jews', the Messiah. This would mark a new beginning for God's People, the Jews. It would be like the end of this world and the beginning of a whole new way of life.

The Christians believed that they were already living in this New Age. They believed that all the Jewish hopes had come true in Jesus. They saw his baptism as his anointing as the Messiah, the 'anointed one'.

1. *'Christ' was not Jesus' surname but a title (originally he was called 'Jesus the Christ'). What did this title mean?*
2. *'Son of David' was used as a title for the Messiah. Explain why.*
3. *At Jesus' baptism he was called the Son of God. This was an echo of Psalm 2:7:*

   ' He said to me: "You are my son;
      today I have become your father." '

   This is a Royal Psalm, perhaps used at the enthronement ceremony of new kings, when they were anointed. If the title 'Son of God' at first referred to the kings of Israel, why should it become a title for the Messiah?
4. *Since 'King of the Jews' was also a Messianic title, what might Christians think when they read the story of Jesus being mocked before his death as if he were a king? (Mark 15:16–20)*
5. *Name the specific title for the Messiah used in each of the following references:*
   a) *Mark 3:11*
   b) *Mark 10:47*
   c) *Mark 15:2*

Jesus' temptations

Jesus' baptism was obviously a very moving experience for him, when he felt inspired and chosen by God. He was convinced now that God was his Father in a very special way and that he was called to his service. It was the turning-point in his life. After this, he gave up his work as a local carpenter, or small-time builder, and took up his ministry of preaching and healing.

Before Jesus began his ministry as the Messiah he took time to think things through and work out in his own mind what it all meant. Where better to go than to the desert? Here he could be alone with his thoughts. We are told that Jesus stayed there for forty days during which time he was tempted by the devil. Matthew and Luke give more details, saying that Jesus went without food all this time and describing three particular temptations that Jesus overcame. Some religious people still practise fasting (going without food for a time) to discipline their bodies so that they can concentrate their minds on something important. Jesus had to think and pray about Messiahship. It would not have been surprising for Jesus to think of himself as the Messiah (every Jewish mother hoped and prayed that her son would be the Messiah). The difficulty was for Jesus to know what God expected of him. The idea had been around for so long that there were many different views about the Messiah. Some people had in mind some sort of supernatural being; others expected a political leader. In Jesus' three temptations he is tempted to misuse his Messianic power to satisfy physical needs, especially his own; to gain political influence; and to prove himself miraculously to the people. Jesus relied on his knowledge of the Scriptures to help him resist these temptations.

It is interesting to see the parallel between this story and an Old Testament one where the Jews spent forty years in the Wilderness between escaping from Egypt under Moses and reaching the Promised Land. For both, this was a period of testing after a momentous turning-point and to prepare them for what lay ahead. The Jews of the Old Testament were preparing to establish themselves in Israel, but there they failed to live up to God's standards. Christians saw Jesus' temptations as a preparation for the setting up of a New Israel, a new People of God who had a new chance to live in God's ways by following Jesus.

Finally Jesus was ready to begin his ministry, strengthened for more temptations and conflicts with evil which lay ahead.

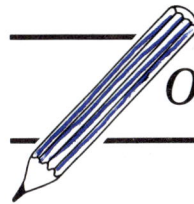

Over to you

1. Are there any events or experiences which you see as a turning-point in your life?
2. Do you like being alone? Explain your answer.
3. When you have important decisions to make, where do you go to work them out?
4. Why do you think the desert has an appeal for some people?
5. Can you think of any situation where you have withstood a temptation to do something wrong?
6. Can you think of any tests which are useful in preparing you to do things in the future? (e.g. Children who want to go rowing or canoeing may have to pass a swimming test first.)
7. Look up Deuteronomy 8:2. What details are similar to the story of Jesus' temptations?
8. Read the full account of Jesus' temptations in Lk 4:1–13 or Mt 4:1–11. Draw a diagram to record these three temptations briefly.
9. Compare Deuteronomy 8:3 with Jesus' first temptation in Luke 4:3–4. What are the words from Deuteronomy after 'man must not depend on bread alone to sustain him'?
10. The Jews thought of the devil as the power of evil. The reference to the devil in this story probably means that evil thoughts came to Jesus. Can you think of any other person or thing which represents evil?

D The desert

Letters from the Desert is a book written by Carlo Carretto. He is a monk who belongs to an order known as the Little Brothers, founded by Charles de Foucauld in the early twentieth century in Algeria. These monks work amongst the very poorest people but their training (their *novitiate*) involves going into the desert to learn to pray. Here are just a few extracts from the book to highlight the importance of this desert experience for these monks.

The great joy of the Saharan novitiate is the solitude, and the joy of solitude — silence, true silence, which penetrates everywhere and invades one's whole being, speaking to the soul with wonderful new strength unknown to men to whom this silence means nothing.

Here, living in perpetual silence, one learns to distinguish its different shades: silence of the church, silence in one's cell, silence at work, interior silence, silence of the soul, God's silence.

To learn to live these silences, the novice-master lets us go away for a few days' 'desert'.

A hamper of bread, a few dates, some water, the Bible. A day's march: a cave.

A priest celebrates Mass; then goes away, leaving in the cave, on an altar of stones, the Eucharist. Thus, for a week one remains alone with the Eucharist exposed day and night. Silence in the desert, silence in the cave, silence in the Eucharist. (*pp. 11—12*) (*NB Being Catholic, the bread and wine of the Eucharist meant that Christ was really present.*)

Let us begin to analyse this element of 'desert'

A remote desert monastery in Egypt. What might the monk be thinking as he gazes towards its walls, amid the vast expanse of desert?

which must be present, especially today, in the carrying out of such a demanding program.

When one speaks of the soul's desert, and says that the desert must be present in your life, you must not think only of the Sahara or the desert of Judea, or into the High Valley of the Nile.

Certainly it is not everyone who can have the advantage of being able to carry out in practice this detachment from daily life. The Lord conducted me into the real desert because I was so thick-skinned. For *me*, it was necessary . . .

But the same way is not for everybody. And if you cannot go into the desert, you must nonetheless 'make some desert' in your life. Every now and then leaving men and looking for solitude to restore, in prolonged silence and prayer, the stuff of your soul. This is the meaning of 'desert' in your spiritual life.

One hour a day, one day a month, eight days a year, for longer if necessary, you must leave everything and everybody and retire, alone with God . . .

But the desert is not the final stopping place. It is a stage on the journey . . .

For me, this is quite costly. The desire to continue living here in the Sahara for ever is so strong that I am already suffering in anticipation of the order that will certainly come from my superiors: 'Brother Charles, leave for Marseilles, leave for Morocco, leave for Venezuela, leave for Detroit.

'You must go back among men, mix with them, live your intimacy with God in the noise of their cities. It will be difficult but you must do it . . .'

Certainly it would be easier and more pleasant to stay here in the desert. But God doesn't seem to want that. (*pp. 72–5*)

In the Foreward, Ivan Illich sums up an important message of the book:

The emptiness of the desert makes it possible to learn the almost impossible: the joyful acceptance of our uselessness. (*p. x*)

1. *What is the first word that comes to mind when you think of deserts?*
2. *What is the main word used about the desert by Brother Charles, in the first extract?*
3. *In the second extract, what does he mean by saying that people must 'make some desert' in their lives?*
4. *Why should the emptiness of the desert (in contrast to built-up areas) make us aware of man's uselessness?*
5. *How would you feel if you were all alone, with desert stretching away in all directions as far as you could see?*

E The Suffering Servant

There are four poems in the Book of the Prophet Isaiah, in the Old Testament, which speak of God's servant. The longest and greatest of these (Isaiah 52:13–53:12) has given rise to the title 'the Suffering Servant'. It speaks of the servant of the Lord who nobly endured suffering and death for the sake of others. Because of this, he is promised future glory. We cannot be sure to whom this 'servant' originally referred. It could have been the prophet himself; or it could have been a collective title for all the faithful Jews who had suffered to preserve Judaism; or it could refer to the future Messiah.

It was in the Messianic sense that it was understood by Christians, and perhaps by Jesus himself. For instance, Matthew quotes the whole of the first Servant Song (Isaiah 42:1–4) to explain why Jesus asked for secrecy from the people he healed:

'Here is my servant, whom I have chosen,
  the one I love and with whom I am pleased.
I will send my Spirit upon him,
  and he will announce my judgment to the nations.
He will not argue or shout,
  or make loud speeches in the streets.
He will not break off a bent reed,

BALLYCLARE HIGH SCHOOL

or put out a flickering lamp.
He will persist until he causes justice to
    triumph,
and in him all peoples will put their hope.'
(Matthew 12:18–21, author's italics, latest
edition)

Jesus taught his disciples the importance
of humble service, both in his words to them
and by his own example. He told them this:

'If one of you wants to be great, he must be the
servant of the rest; and if one of you wants to be
first, he must be the slave of all. For even the Son
of Man did not come to be served; he came to
serve and to give his life to redeem many people.'
(Mark 10:43–5)

Jesus demonstrated this in John's Gospel by
washing his own disciples' feet.
    It was with the death of Jesus, and the trial
scenes beforehand, that the early Christians
saw the closest connections with the Suffering Servant. This is from one of Peter's
speeches:

'The God of our ancestors has given divine
glory to his Servant Jesus. But you handed him
over to the authorities, and you rejected him in
Pilate's presence.' (Acts 3:13)

Another incident also comes from the Book
of the Acts of the Apostles, where a foreigner
was riding along in his carriage, reading
aloud from one of the Servant Songs. The
passage from Isaiah 53:7–8 is quoted:

'Like a sheep that is taken to be slaughtered,
    like a lamb that makes no sound when its wool
    is cut off,
    he did not say a word.
He was humiliated, and justice was denied him.
    No one will be able to tell about his
    descendants,
    because his life on earth has come to an end.'
(Acts 8:32–3)

Philip, a leading member of the church in
Jerusalem, came across him and asked if he
understood what he was reading. Then Philip
explained it to him in terms of Jesus' death,
and preached the gospel to him. The man was
so impressed that he became a Christian. As
soon as they came across some water the
man ordered his carriage to stop and he was
baptized by Philip to show that he had converted to Christianity.

*Christians identify Jesus with the Suffering Ser-
vant, spoken of in the Old Testament. Here Jesus
is shown washing the disciples' feet — doing the
servant's job. When you have read the story from
John 13, you will be able to guess which disciple
is in the front of the picture.*

1. *Read the story of the washing of the disciples'
    feet in John 13:3–5 and 12–17:*
    a) *Briefly tell the story in your own words.*
    b) *Illustrate it.*
    c) *Explain why Jesus did it.*
    d) *Think of some unexpected act of humility
        that someone in authority today could do to
        teach the same lesson.*
2. *Compare the first three lines of the Servant
    Song quoted above from Matthew 12 with the
    words spoken to Jesus from heaven at his bap-
    tism (see Mark 1:11). How are they similar?*
3. *Look up Mark 14:61a and 15:5 from the
    account of Jesus' trials. What is similar in the
    Servant Song quoted above, from Isaiah 53?*

'You are the Messiah'

The first time in the Gospels that Jesus is openly and quite plainly called the Messiah is an important incident involving the disciples. They had now been with Jesus for some time, witnessing all that he did, and doing similar things themselves. One day Jesus asked them who people thought he was. A number of different answers were given. Then he asked: 'What about you? Who do you say I am?' Simon Peter, acting as the spokesman for the rest of them, said, 'You are the Messiah.' Jesus' first reaction was to tell them to keep it secret, perhaps because he was afraid that people would misunderstand.

Now that his disciples had recognised him as the Messiah, he had to explain to them more fully what this meant. Using the title he preferred, he explained that the Son of Man would have to suffer before coming into his glory. Peter's reaction shows that even the disciples had not realised what sort of Messiah Jesus was. He grabbed Jesus by the arm, arguing that this could not be right. The idea of suffering just did not fit into Peter's picture of the Messiah. Jesus' reaction to Peter was very harsh: 'Get away from me, Satan,' he said. 'Your thoughts don't come from God but from man!' (Mark 8:33) This was just like the earlier temptations in the wilderness, tempting Jesus to follow the popular idea of Messiahship and take the easy way out. Jesus went on to teach his disciples that they too must be prepared to suffer.

Soon after this episode Jesus went off with his closest disciples, Peter, James and John. He took them up a mountain where they had a strange experience which convinced them that Jesus was right about his Messiahship. They saw a vision of Jesus with a radiant appearance. With him were two great Old Testament figures: Moses the law-giver and Elijah the prophet. Luke says they were talking with Jesus about his coming death in Jerusalem. Just as Jesus had heard God speaking to him at his baptism, assuring him that he was the Messiah, so now the disciples heard God speak to them about Jesus, in similar words: 'This is my own dear Son — listen to him!' (Mark 9:7)

What meaning did the Gospel writers see in this story? Moses and Elijah represented Judaism, especially the Jewish Scriptures which consisted mainly of the Laws of Moses and the Books of the Prophets. So this vision meant that Jesus was fulfilling the promises God made to the Jews in their Bible, and that he had understood God's plan correctly — that the Messiah must suffer. There is also another meaning in the presence of Elijah, when we remember that Elijah was supposed to return before the Messiah. This story of the Transfiguration would satisfy some early Christians who had wondered where Elijah was, if Jesus was the Messiah. Others thought of John the Baptist as the new Elijah.

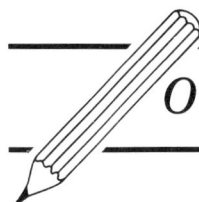

Over to you

1. Jesus' idea of the Messiah was very different from that which the disciples had been brought up with. What do you think they expected of a powerful and glorious Messiah?
2. This song from the rock musical *Jesus Christ Superstar* shows that Jesus had a different idea of power and glory. Try to write some more lyrics to this song, explaining that the Messiah would only achieve victory through suffering.

   Neither you Simon, nor the fifty thousand,
   nor the Romans, nor the Jews,
   nor Judas, nor the Twelve,
   nor the priests, nor the scribes,
   nor doomed Jerusalem itself,
   understand what power is —
   understand what glory is —
   understand at all.
   . . . .
   To conquer death you only have to die —
   you only have to die. (*Lyrics by Tim Rice*)

'Then a cloud appeared and covered them with its shadow, and a voice came from the cloud, "This is my own dear Son — listen to him!"' (Mark 9:7)

3. Why did Jesus call Peter 'Satan'?
4. What did 'the Law and the Prophets' refer to in Judaism?
5. Read Matthew 17:9–13. Who is identified with Elijah here?

Art work

Illustrate a scene from one of the following stories, for display:
a) Jesus' baptism
b) Jesus' temptations
c) Jesus' transfiguration.
Remember that these stories were meant to show Jesus as the Messiah.

Important words

Check the meaning of the following words by looking them up in the Word list at the back of this book. This is the order in which they occur in Part 2:

prophet/prophecy	**ritual**
Judaism	**Church**
to repent	**Messianic**
sin	**Christ**
to baptize/baptism	**temptation**
monastery/monastic	**Satan**
symbol	

Make sure you can spell
prophet (not profit, which is to do with money)
baptism (there is no 'u' in it)
monastery (notice the 'e')
religious (notice the second 'i')

F The Son of Man

Jesus does not seem to have gone around making direct claims to be the Messiah. This was probably because he was afraid people would have the wrong ideas about the Messiah. Instead he used the title 'Son of Man' for himself. This appears in the Old Testament but does not seem to have been in general use as a title for the Messiah.

The Hebrew phrase *son of man* originally just meant 'man' or 'everyman', like the English phrase 'every mother's son'. It did not refer to anyone special, in fact the opposite, it meant anyone and everyone.

It became a special title in the Book of Daniel, the last Old Testament book to have been written. The Book of Daniel contains strange visions and it has this description of the Son of Man:

I saw in the night visions,
and behold, with the clouds of heaven
   there came one like a son of man,
and he came to the Ancient of Days
   and was presented before him.
And to him was given dominion
   and glory and kingdom,
that all peoples, nations, and languages
   should serve him;
his dominion is an everlasting dominion,
   which shall not pass away,
and his kingdom one

that shall not be destroyed.
(Daniel 7:13–14, *RSV*)

When Daniel asks what this vision means, he is told that the 'Saints of the Most High' will receive the kingdom and rule for ever. The Book of Daniel was written to encourage the Jews of the second century BC to hold firm to their faith in the face of persecution. There had been many martyrs, and these 'Saints of the Most High' are promised an everlasting reward. Son of Man here refers not to just one person but to all the faithful Jews.

We do not know why Jesus took this title 'Son of Man'. Was it to identify himself with all humanity and to show that he represented everyone? Or was it because the Saints of the Most High/Son of Man had suffered before being rewarded with everlasting glory? In the same way, Jesus turned his back on all the worldly advantages that he might have had as the Messiah, believing instead that God wanted him to make sacrifices and to endure suffering.

1. *Copy out the references to the Son of Man from the following verses:*
   a) Mark 2:10 (or Luke 5:24)
   b) Mark 2:28 (or Luke 6:5)
   c) Mark 14:62 (or Luke 22:69)

Part 3 The Kingdom

The Kingdom of God

Just as the Jews thought of the Messiah as a king, so they spoke of the time of salvation which the Messiah would bring as a kingdom. Children brought up in Christian countries are familiar with this idea, from the Lord's Prayer:

Our Father, who art in heaven,
hallowed be thy name;
thy kingdom come;
thy will be done;
on earth as it is in heaven...

This prayer was taught by Jesus to his disciples. As Jews, they would have known a prayer with some similar words:

May he establish his kingdom
    During your life
    And during your days,
    And during the life of all the house of
        Israel,
Even speedily and at a near time,
And say ye, Amen.

We use the word 'kingdom' to describe a place — a country ruled by a monarch. The United Kingdom, for instance, is England, Wales, Scotland and Northern Ireland, all of which countries are ruled by Queen Elizabeth II. Perhaps then 'kingdom' is the wrong word to translate this Jewish image of the Kingdom of God, because it did not mean for them a particular place. The word 'kingship' would be better because the Kingdom of God was really describing the reign of God. It was a picture of the time when all people would accept God's rule over the world he had created. The Jews longed for the time when the Messiah would come to establish God's kingship on earth and change this wicked world into a heavenly place in which to live. There are many poetic descriptions of this imaginary new world in their Scriptures:

Wolves and sheep will live together in peace,
    and leopards will lie down with young goats.
Calves and lion cubs will feed together,
    and little children will take care of them.
Cows and bears will eat together,
    and their calves and cubs will lie down in
        peace.
Lions will eat straw as cattle do.
Even a baby will not be harmed
    if it plays near a poisonous snake.
On Zion, God's sacred hill,
    there will be nothing harmful or evil.
The land will be as full of knowledge of the
    LORD
    as the seas are full of water.
(Isaiah 11:6—9)

The message in the Gospels is that the Messiah had come in the person of Jesus and he had already begun to establish the Kingdom of God. Those who responded to Jesus and followed the rule of God which he taught were regarded as the new citizens of this Kingdom. Mark says:

After John had been put in prison, Jesus went to Galilee and preached the Good News from God. 'The right time has come,' he said, 'and the Kingdom of God is near! Turn away from your sins and believe the Good News!' (Mark 1:14—15)

Jesus preached the good news that the New Age had arrived. Christians proclaimed the good news that it had arrived in the person of Jesus. They wrote the Gospels ('Good News') to record this belief and to give their evidence for it.

NB Matthew's Gospel speaks of the Kingdom of Heaven rather than the Kingdom of God. It meant the same thing but, being brought up as a good Jew, Matthew did not like to say the name of God. It was considered too holy.

1. What is another way of saying 'Kingdom of God'? What does it mean?
2. Make up your own poem to describe your dream world of the future.

3. Look up the following references and copy out what they have to say about the Kingdom of God:
   a) Luke 9:27
   b) Luke 10:9
   c) Luke 11:2
   d) Luke 11:20
   e) Luke 17:20-1

A Parables

Jesus preached his message to the people, using many other parables like these; he told them as much as they could understand. (Mark 4:33)

The word 'parable' means 'to put beside' or 'to compare' and it describes a type of story which has a parallel meaning that you could put alongside it. These stories were not fanciful fairy-tales but were taken from everyday life. Many of Jesus' parables are about the farmers and fishermen of Galilee where he lived. The old explanation of parables is quite a good one: 'A parable is an earthly story with a heavenly meaning.'

Some parables are very short, just a line or two, like this one:

' The Kingdom of heaven is like this. A woman takes some yeast and mixes it with forty litres of flour until the whole batch of dough rises. ' (Matthew 13:33)

Or they may even be as short as this:

' People who are well do not need a doctor, but only those who are sick. '

This is followed by its parallel meaning:

' I have not come to call respectable people to repent, but outcasts. ' (Luke 5:31-2)

Other parables of Jesus are long stories, like the famous Parable of the Prodigal Son which takes up twenty-one verses in Luke 15.

A parable usually has only one main point to make. So the smaller details of the story are not important in themselves, and it is likely that these changed a little as the parable was retold. The details only serve to make the story realistic, to keep the hearers' attention and to help put over the central meaning of the parable.

The Jews were used to parables. The prophets had used them hundreds of years before, and some of these are recorded in the Old Testament. In Jesus' day, the Jewish religious teachers (called _rabbis_) often put across a point in this vivid and memorable way. Jesus was by no means the first or only person to teach in parables, but he certainly seems to have made good use of this method. Many of his parables were remembered and recorded in the Gospels.

1. _What do you think the Parable of the Yeast means? (The emphasis is on the_ small _amount of yeast that is needed to make a_ large _amount of dough rise, when making bread.)_
2. _Read the parable told by the prophet Isaiah in Isaiah 5:1-7 and copy out verse 7, which gives its meaning._
3. _Think of as many reasons as possible why Jesus may have used parables, especially when teaching the crowds. (Imagine the situation of Jesus preaching in the open air to large numbers of people, many of whom were uneducated. You will also need to look back carefully over what is said about parables in this section.)_

Parables of the Kingdom

Jesus' message was about salvation, 'the Kingdom of God'; and he often taught in stories called parables, (see section A). Many of these parables about the Kingdom have been preserved in the Gospels. If we look at some of them, we shall get an idea of what Jesus taught.

The Parable of the Lamp

(Mt 5:15; Mk 4:21; Lk 11:33) This parable says that you do not light a lamp and then cover it up, but you put it on a lampstand to make the most of its light. In the same way, Christians had been given the gospel and it was their job to spread this good news to others. Luke had remembered the Old Testament passage which prophesied that the Messiah would bring light to the Gentiles as well as being the saviour of the Jews. He says the lamp is 'so that people may see the light as they come in', suggesting those who came into the Kingdom from outside of Judaism.

Light is an important symbol in religions. This shows a girl putting a votive candle into a special holder, in church. 'Votive' means 'offering': the candles are bought and lit as an offering to God.

The Parable of the Lost Sheep

(Mt 18:10; Lk 15:1) This teaches that it is not just the holy people who are welcome in the Kingdom but also sinners. It tells of a shepherd who has a hundred sheep. If even one of them gets lost, he will leave the rest to go in search of the lost sheep until he finds it. Then he will carry it home and celebrate with his friends, for he is so delighted to have found the one that was lost. Many religious Jews of Jesus' day felt that *they* deserved to enter God's Kingdom, but not others. Yet Jesus had a lot of time for the less religious people, the 'lost sheep', showing the religious people that they should be glad when sinners repented and were saved. In Matthew's Gospel Jesus claimed to have been sent to 'the lost sheep of the house of Israel'.

An Indian painting of Jesus as the Good Shepherd.

The Parable of the Mustard Seed

(Mt 13:31; Mk 4:30; Lk 13:18) This tells how the tiniest of seeds grows into a big bush whose branches give shade to the birds. This sums it all up: the Kingdom was started by Jesus and his small band of followers, but it would grow into a big movement, capable of taking in any number and variety of people, whether Jew or Gentile, saint or sinner. By the end of the first century, Christianity had indeed spread beyond the land of the Jews, throughout the whole Roman (i.e. Gentile) world.

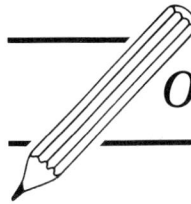

Over to you

1. The image of light is found in most religions to represent the spiritual enlightenment that it is thought religion can bring. Can you think of any examples of lights, like candles, being used as symbols in religions?
2. What image for Jesus is used in John 8:12?
3. We use lights for two main reasons:
   a) to help us see things more clearly, and
   b) to lead us in the dark and bring us safely to our destination.
   Give examples of these two uses of light from everyday life.
4. With the same two uses of light in mind, explain how Christians can speak of the Gospel as light.
5. Look up Isaiah 9:2 and Luke 2:32 and copy out the phrases which express the idea that the light of God's salvation would come to the Gentiles.
6. What does the Parable of the Lamp teach Christians to do?
7. What image for Jesus is used in John 10:11?
8. What does the Parable of the Lost Sheep teach about God?
9. A similar parable to the Lost Sheep, with the same meaning, is found in Luke 15:8–10. What was lost in this story?
10. Read a similar parable to the Mustard Seed in Ezekiel 17:22–3. What tree is used in the imagery in this parable? (The topmost branch represents the House of David and the tender shoot taken from it is the Messiah.)

Jesus' message had a note of urgency in it. One parable after another drove home the warning that they were living at the eleventh hour. Now was the time for people to accept the invitation to enter God's Kingdom — before it was too late.

The Parable of the Pearl of Great Price

This parable teaches that salvation (the Kingdom) is the most important thing in life. It is worth giving up everything else for. The parable is short enough to be quoted here in full:

> 'Also, the Kingdom of heaven is like this. A man is looking for fine pearls, and when he finds one that is unusually fine, he goes and sells everything he has, and buys that pearl.' (Matthew 13:45-6)

The Parable of the Rich Man and Lazarus

(Lk 16:19) This is the story of a rich man who lives in the lap of luxury while ignoring Lazarus, a poor man who begs at his gate. The contrast between the lives of the two men is drawn out. Lazarus is the only named character in any of Jesus' parables that we have. This suggests that we are to see some meaning in his name, which meant 'God is his help'. Probably Lazarus represents the righteous poor people who trust in God, and who are shown in Luke's Gospel to be God's special concern.

When the two men in the story die, Lazarus goes to heaven whilst the rich man goes to hell. In agony, he cries out to Abraham for pity, asking that Lazarus be sent with some cool water to ease his torment in the fires of hell. Abraham points out that they each have what they deserve: poor Lazarus had previously gone hungry and now he is at peace; but the rich man had already had his time of happiness. 'Besides all that,' says Abraham, 'there is a deep pit lying between us, so that those who want to cross over from here to you cannot do so, nor can anyone cross over to us from where you are.'

Seeing that it is too late to save himself, the rich man asks Lazarus to warn his five brothers who are still alive, so that they at least might be saved. He thinks that, although they pay no attention to the warnings in their Scriptures (the Books of Moses and the Prophetic Books), they would be sure to change their ways if they saw Lazarus. Abraham answers: 'If they will not listen to Moses and the prophets, they will not be convinced even if someone were to rise from death.'

This message of this parable is that people should heed the warnings of judgment before it is too late. It finishes on an important note because Luke believed that people had *both* the Scriptures *and* the proof of someone come back from the dead. Yet still people ignored the Good News that Jesus was the Messiah and the message that he taught. This parable is a warning to such people that they will find themselves on the wrong side of the gulf, so to speak, if they do not watch out.

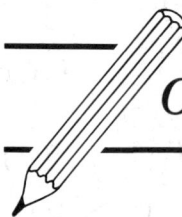

Over to you

1. What does the Parable of the Pearl of Great Price teach about the importance of salvation?
2. Look up Matthew 13:44 where there is a similar parable to the one about the pearl. What takes the place of the pearl in this parable?
3. Write your own short parable, similar to the one about the pearl and with the same meaning.
4. Look up Luke 6:20—6. What does it say there about the poor and the rich?
5. Why do you think there is a preference for the poor in the Bible, rather than for the rich?
6. Can you think of any reasons why poor people might be more religious than rich people? (Consider the meaning of the name 'Lazarus' and the New Testament saying, 'The love of money is the root of all evil.')
7. The Gospel writers believed that someone had really come back from death. Whom did they mean?

B Heaven and Hell

It was not the purpose of the Parable of the Rich Man and Lazarus to describe in detail what happens to people after death; rather, it was a warning to respond to God in this life. Yet it paints a picture of life after death which made sense to the Jews of those days and to the early Christians.

In Old Testament times there was little idea of personal survival after death. Most people seem to have believed in a shadowy

These panels are from a painting called 'The Last Judgment'. They show us how Christians used to think of heaven and hell 500 years ago. Which panel shows heaven? In what direction are the for-tunate people going? Who are the creatures with wings? Which panel shows hell? In what direction are the unfortunate people going? What symbol of hell can you see there?

world of the dead, called *Sheol* in Hebrew, and later called *Hades* (Greek) in New Testament times. They thought of it as a deep pit under the earth. At the very end of the Old Testament period (about 165 BC), there emerged the idea that those Jews who had died for their faith would be rewarded with everlasting life at the future Day of Judgment. This developed so that by New Testament times there were various places spoken of where the wicked and righteous were supposed to be separated after death as they awaited the final judgment. For example, Paradise was a pleasant place to be in, and came to be referred to as *Heaven* in later Christianity; and Gehenna was a terrifying place, and came to be called *Hell*.

If you visit Jerusalem, you can see a place called the Valley of Hinnom, just outside the city. In Old Testament times this was used as the city's rubbish tip, and there·would often be fires burning there. The fires of the Valley of Hinnom also had a more sinister connection. There had been times in their early history (between 1000 and 600 BC) when the Jews had turned to pagan gods. In times of extreme need they had burned children as sacrifices to the god, Molech, on this site. The fires in the Valley of Hinnom — called *Gehenna* in Greek — became the image for hell, with its fiery torments.

Not all Jews accepted these new ideas. The Sadducees, for instance, only believed what was written in the first five books of the Bible, the earliest part. But Jesus believed in life after death.

These Jewish ideas came into Christianity along with some new thoughts on the subject. John's Gospel, for example, emphasises the belief that 'eternal life' (life with God) can already be experienced in this earthly life, and will go on beyond death. St Paul also taught that Christians will be raised to a new spiritual life after death, since Jesus had risen from the dead. The Roman Catholic Church teaches that there is another stage, between earth and heaven, called *Purgatory*. Here souls are believed to be purged, or purified, and made ready for heaven. Some modern Christians have played down the notion of hell, because they believe that God will never give up on those he has created and loves. Others say that the old pictures of heaven and hell may now sound silly, but the warnings they give about turning our backs on God are just as serious as they ever were.

There is a well-known parable about heaven and hell which comes from Korea. It tells of someone who died and was taken to heaven but, before entering, he asked if he might be taken on a conducted tour of hell. What he saw amazed him at first, for there was a big table, piled high with food. But everyone there was starving because they had been given five-foot-long chopsticks, with the instructions that they had to use them if they wanted any food, and they had to hold them at the ends. What torment these people were in, seeing all this delicious food, but being unable to get it to their mouths. Then the Korean and his escort returned to heaven and there the situation was just the same: a table laden with food and all the people with five-foot-long chopsticks and the same instructions. Yet these people were not starving like the others; they were well-fed, happy and all getting on well with each other.

Can you see how those in heaven worked it out? They fed each other!

1. *What pictures do you have in your mind when you hear the words 'heaven' and 'hell'?*
2. *What do you believe happens to us when our bodies die?*
3. *Read St Paul's explanation of life after death in I Corinthians 15:12–15, 35–44 and 50–7.*
   a) On what does he base his belief in life after death?
   b) What parable does he use to illustrate the connection between this life and the next?
4. *What do you think is meant by the idea of 'hell on earth'?*
5. *What do you think the Korean parable means?*
6. *Write a poem with the lines of one verse beginning with the words 'Heaven is _____' and the lines of the other verse beginning 'Hell is _____'*

The Parable of the Darnel

(Mt 13:24) This may have been told to answer the critics who asked why the world had not changed dramatically if the Kingdom was supposed to have come.

The story is of a farmer who sowed a field of corn; but at dead of night his enemy planted darnel, a grassy weed, among it. Both types of plant sprouted up together but the farmer dared not pull up the weeds for fear of damaging the growing corn. He would wait until harvest time and then gather the darnel first, to be burnt, and then the corn, to be stored in his barn.

Wheat   Darnel

The answer to the critics was that Satan was still at work in the world but, although evil people did what they could to destroy God's Kingdom, they would not succeed and in the end each would get what he deserved.

The Christians themselves must have been puzzled by this question of why the Kingdom of God was not now plainly established for all to see. Many of the parables, like the Mustard Seed, gave them encouragement. These parables showed them that it was early days yet and the Kingdom was still growing. Christians believed that the Kingdom had started quietly, almost secretly, and that they were living in the time of its growth; but they looked forward to a time when the Kingdom would be completed. Many early Christians spoke of this in the visionary language which was common amongst the Jews of that time. They thought in terms of Christ descending on the clouds of heaven, coming in glory at the end of the world, on the dreadful Day of Judgment. Many early Christians mistakenly thought this would happen in their own lifetime.

The Parable of the Sheep and the Goats

(Mt 25:31) This parable speaks of this Last Day. It opens with these words:

'When the Son of Man comes as King and all the angels with him, he will sit on his royal throne, and the people of all the nations will be gathered before him.' (Matthew 25:31–2)

The story goes on to say that the King will separate the people into two groups — like a shepherd separates the sheep from the goats at the end of the day: the sheep on his right hand and the goats on his left. The King will reward those on his right with a place in his kingdom. He will explain that they deserve this because of the way they have lived. He will say:

'I was hungry and you fed me, thirsty and you gave me a drink; I was a stranger and you received me in your homes, naked and you clothed me; I was sick and you took care of me, in prison and you visited me.' (25:35–6)

The righteous will admit that they could not remember ever having done anything for the King; and he will explain:

'I tell you, whenever you did this for one of the least important of these brothers of mine, you did it for me!' (25:40)

Then those on the left will be accused of refusing to help the King, because whenever they ignored someone in need it was like ignoring the King himself.

The King, of course, is meant to be the Messiah, Jesus Christ. The story teaches that in serving others, people are serving Christ himself, and that people will be judged by the way they have lived.

Jesus told parables from everyday life. He would have often seen a shepherd with his sheep.

Over to you

1. In the Parable of the Darnel, what are we meant to think of when we hear that, at harvest time, the darnel will be thrown on a fire?
2. Fire is an image of hell because it is frightening and it destroys evil. Give an example from everyday life of how fire can
   a) cause pain, and
   b) destroy something which is regarded as unwanted, nasty or even dangerous.
3. Read out dramatically in class the Parable of the Sheep and the Goats. You will find it in Matthew 25:31–46. You will need one person for the narrator, another for the King, and the rest of the class can be divided into the sheep and the goats.

Art work

Choose any one of the parables in Part 3 and illustrate it on a piece of paper for display.

Important words

Check the meaning of the following words by looking them up in the Word list at the back of this book. This is the order in which they occur in Part 3:

Kingdom of God/Heaven	**Gentile**
parable	**material**
repentance	**spiritual**
rabbi	**righteous**
salvation	

C

'When I needed a neighbour'

This well-known song is based on words from the Parable of the Sheep and the Goats.

1 When I needed a neighbour were you there, were you there?
When I needed a neighbour were you there?
And the creed and the colour and the name won't matter,
Were you there?

2 I was hungry and thirsty, were you there, were you there? . . .

3 I was cold, I was naked, were you there, were you there? . . .

4 When I needed a shelter were you there, were you there? . . .

5 When I needed a healer were you there, were you there? . . .

6 Wherever you travel I'll be there, I'll be there,
Wherever you travel I'll be there.
And the creed and the colour and the name won't matter
I'll be there.

D

Judaism

Jews are the followers of a religion which is still alive today, called Judaism. They claim that it goes back almost 4,000 years to their ancestor Abraham who first believed in the one God. Jews still follow many of the beliefs and laws laid down by Moses, a great leader who lived about 500 years after Abraham. The Jewish people have survived many setbacks over their long history and their religion has continued to develop into the present day.

One of the biggest blows came in about 600 BC when enemies destroyed their capital city of Jerusalem and the holy Temple there. Yet the Jews managed to survive this defeat and the exile that followed it. When they returned to their land of Israel, they rebuilt the Temple and followed their religion with renewed zeal. They decided that from then on they would try to keep their laws, and, when they did wrong, their priests would offer

sacrifices for them in the Temple so that God would never again have to punish them for their sins. So the Judaism that Jesus knew, in the first century AD, was a religion ruled to a large extent by the priesthood from the Temple in Jerusalem, headed by the High Priest; and it was based on the Scriptures, particularly the law books, known as the Books of Moses.

Some developments in the second century BC had also made a difference to the Judaism of Jesus' day. This period saw a great surge of Jewish patriotism and, as well as outright rebellion against their Greek rulers, there was also a move to keep their religion more strictly, so that they were not tempted to follow Greek ideas. It was at this time that the Pharisees emerged as a group of very religious Jews, and that the synagogues became popular as regular places of worship where the ordinary people could take part in the services.

Not long after Jesus' life, in AD 70, there came another very serious blow to Judaism. This time, Jerusalem and the Temple were destroyed by the Romans, after the Jews had revolted. The Temple was not rebuilt and, without it, any priests who were left alive became redundant. Gradually the priesthood and the whole business of sacrifices disappeared from Judaism. The Judaism that remained by the end of the first century AD was the religion of the Pharisees. It was a religion concerned with living by the laws of Judaism and worshipping God regularly in the synagogues.

Jesus was a practising Jew who worshipped in a synagogue, often taking a leading part by reading the set passage from the Scriptures and preaching the sermon. His first followers were also Jews and his mission was to Israel. The Jewish Scriptures were used by the first Christians, who later called them the *Old Testament* when they made them part of the Christian Bible.

Jews are not especially interested in Jesus. They know that he existed, of course, but they do not think that he was the Messiah. They are still waiting for the Messiah. They do not think that they threw away their chance of salvation by rejecting Jesus. They think of Jesus as a self-appointed Jewish teacher who, like many other Jews of that time, was executed by the Romans as a rebel. They think that Christians were misguided in forming a new religion to follow Jesus.

The attitude of Jews towards Christianity is much the same as the attitude of Christians towards the religion of Islam. About six hundred years after Jesus there lived another great religious figure, Muhammad, the leader of Islam. Muslims, the followers of this religion, claim that Muhammad was greater than Abraham, Moses or Jesus. They claim that he was the last and greatest of all the prophets sent by God to teach people the best way to live. Muslims claim that their holy book, the Qur'an, is perfect and is much better than the Christian Bible or the Jewish Scriptures. The religions of Judaism, Christianity and Islam all worship the one God and have much else in common; but each, in turn, claims to be right. Although there may be understanding and even admiration of the different religions, the fact remains that Jews do not accept the claims made by Christians about Jesus, and Christians and Jews do not accept the claims made by Muslims about Muhammad.

The seven-branched candlestick is a symbol of Judaism because there used to be one in the Temple. This sculpture was given to the State of Israel by the British government and stands opposite its parliament building.

Jesus' miracles

All the Gospels include stories of miracles that Jesus performed, many of them healing miracles. Like most other things for the Jews of

This is from a mosaic in the Cathedral of Monreale, Sicily. It shows a paralysed man, a blind man and a cripple who have come to Jesus for healing.

first-century Palestine, medicine came under religious laws. Illness was seen as a punishment from God for sin, and recovery was something for which to thank him. Take the example of a leprosy sufferer who recovered from his skin disease. He would have to get the priest's permission before returning home and mixing with healthy people again; and the priest would make sacrifices for him at the Temple in Jerusalem. Other religious leaders, the rabbis, issued licences for doctors and surgeons to practise in the towns. For common complaints, most people no doubt preferred to use traditional herbal remedies rather than spend money on doctor's fees. There were also faith-healers who cured people's illnesses through their minds. In those days this was often mixed up with belief in demon-possession, and these wonder-workers could put on spectacular performances of casting out devils in order to restore people to good health and sanity.

It must have been Jesus' remarkable healing powers that attracted many people to him in the first place and proved to people that he was special. The Gospel writers certainly saw these miracles as signs that God was working through Jesus. To them, Jesus was no ordinary wonder-worker, out to make a name for himself, but someone who performed miracles through the power of God. Remember Peter's sermon (page 12)? He proclaimed:

'Jesus of Nazareth was a man whose divine authority was clearly proven to you by all the miracles and wonders which God performed through him. You yourselves know this, for it happened here among you.' (Acts 2:22)

Jesus' miracles were connected with his teaching that the Kingdom of God had begun and that God's power was already at work in the world. In an argument over the casting out of evil spirits (not whether Jesus could do it, but by what power), Jesus said:

'No, it is rather by means of God's power that I drive out demons, and this proves that the Kingdom of God has already come to you.' (Luke 11:20)

While John the Baptist was in prison, he began to question whether Jesus really was the Messiah after all. So he sent some of his disciples to Jesus to ask him outright. Jesus did not reply straight away, for he was busy healing the sick. Then he gave them this answer:

'Go back and tell John what you have seen and heard: the blind can see, the lame can walk, those who suffer from dreaded skin-diseases are made clean, the deaf can hear, the dead are raised to life, and the Good News is preached to the poor. How happy are those who have no doubts about me!' (Luke 7:22–3)

This answer is clear enough: Jesus had proved his special powers by demonstrating them. Yet there was more to this answer than meets the eye. Jesus was using biblical language, from passages which the Jews understood to refer to the Messiah (see section A).

So it was important for the Gospel writers to record stories of Jesus restoring sight to the blind, healing cripples, cleansing lepers, making the deaf hear and raising the dead. They saw these as clear signs of his Messiahship.

Over to you

1. Can you name any traditional types of medicine which are becoming respectable again in our modern age? (e.g. What is the name of the Chinese treatment whereby long needles are inserted into the body and rotated?)
2. Do you know of any herbal remedies that are still used today? (Many can be bought in Health Food Shops, e.g. herbal teas of different sorts.)
3. Do you know of any traditional remedies for common complaints like colds and bruises? (e.g. In the second verse of the nursery rhyme, *Jack and Jill*, how was Jack's bumped head treated?)
4. Look up Luke 10:34:
   a) Find out what could be used to cleanse wounds, and what could be used to soothe and heal them, in Jesus' day.
   b) Name a medical product that you could buy today to do each of these two things.
5. Why were Jesus' miracles so important to the Gospel writers?
6. Why then do you think many people who saw Jesus perform miracles did *not* accept him as the Messiah?

A | Prophecies about the Messiah

Isaiah 29:18–19:

When that day comes, the deaf will be able to hear a book being read aloud, and the blind, who have been living in darkness, will open their eyes and see. Poor and humble people will once again find the happiness which the LORD, the holy God of Israel, gives.

Isaiah 35:5–6:

The blind will be able to see,
  and the deaf will hear.
The lame will leap and dance,
  and those who cannot speak will shout for joy.

Isaiah 61:1:

The Sovereign LORD has filled me with his
  spirit.
He has chosen me and sent me
To bring good news to the poor,
To heal the broken-hearted,
To announce release to captives
And freedom to those in prison.

1. *Which of these passages is closest to Jesus' reply in Luke 7:22–3, quoted on this page?*
2. *Which words in the third passage mean 'gospel'? (Look up 'gospel' in the Word list at the back of the book if you cannot remember this.)*

The blind can see

Jesus travelled through Jericho, a lovely oasis town in the midst of the Judaean desert that offers the traveller the cool shade of its palm trees. As usual, people crowded around Jesus and his disciples. Then Jesus heard someone calling again and again: 'Jesus! Son of David! Take pity on me!' It was Bartimaeus, a blind beggar, sitting by the roadside. The people tried to shut him up but he was determined to attract Jesus' attention. Jesus called for the blind man and asked him what he wanted. He replied, 'Teacher, I want to see again.' Jesus restored his sight and told him that his faith had cured him. In other words, Jesus was not a magician, performing tricks on people whether they liked it or not; he could only heal people if they were ready for it and believed that they would be made well. Bartimaeus believed that Jesus was the Messiah, and he became one of his followers.

Over to you

1. If you want to look up this story you can find it in Mark 10:46–52 or Luke 18:35–43.
2. What Messianic title does Bartimaeus use to describe Jesus?
3. Why do you think the other people tried to make Bartimaeus keep quiet?
4. How do we know from the story that Bartimaeus really did believe that Jesus could cure him?
5. *Either* act out this story.
   Or write it up as a play, in your own words.

A street scene in Jericho today.

B The Church's ministry of healing

Many people have heard of the miracles that Jesus is said to have performed long ago, but they may not have come across the Christian belief that similar things can still happen. The 'good news' that Jesus can bring health to mind and body is still proclaimed as the Church continues Jesus' ministry of healing in different ways. This might mean paying for medical research and treatment and/or praying for God's healing power to help individuals. Sometimes special healing services are held.

The following passages are taken from the book *Fear No Evil* by a well-known Christian preacher, David Watson. In recording his own personal struggle with cancer of the colon and liver, he expresses the Christian faith that Christ can overcome the evil of disease.

a Each January, when I am in California as a visiting lecturer at Fuller Theological Seminary, I go whenever possible to a remarkable church called The Vineyard at Yorba Linda, where John Wimber is the main pastor. This church has grown from nothing to 4,000 in four years . . .

What attracts so many to this church? They come in their jeans and T-shirts, and superficially nothing could look less like a typical church service . . . The whole event is wonderfully relaxed and low-key, with nothing of the showbiz performance common in so many of the big American churches. My first impressions there were dominated by the incredible sense of genuine caring love pervading the entire church, together with a gentle spirit of intimate worship . . .

One of the most powerful attractions of the church, however, is to be found in the 'signs and wonders' which happen at every service. After a sustained time of worship, followed by excellent Bible teaching (usually from John Wimber), those who want to find Christ, or who need healing or other help, are invited into a side room. Probably a hundred or more are counselled and prayed for each week. Remarkable healings take place. And it is not just backaches, headaches and toothaches, although those afflictions are no doubt dealt with too. But the blind receive their sight, the deaf hear, the lame walk, those who are

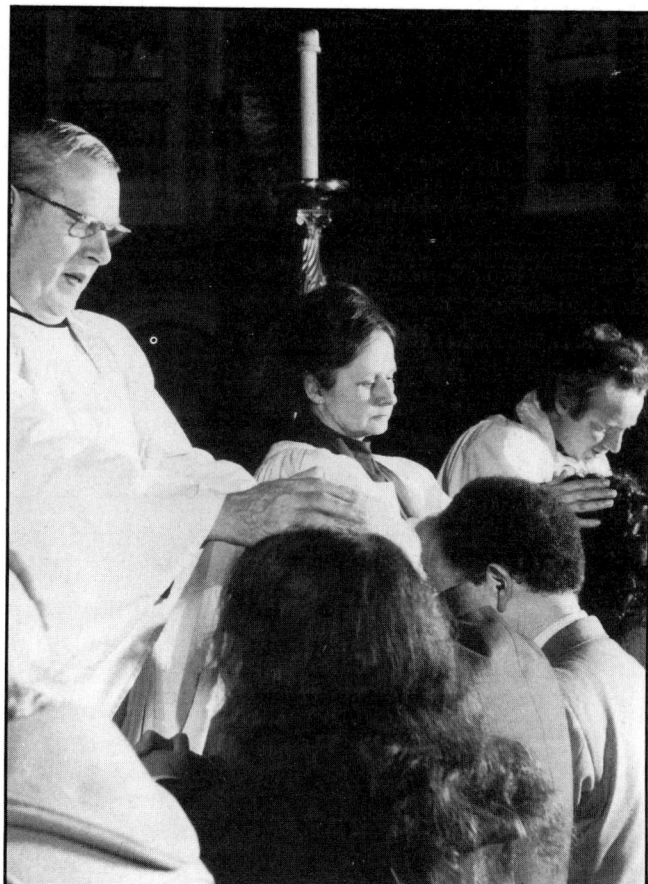

This was taken at a Church of England healing service, and shows the 'laying on of hands'. How can the priest and deaconess be recognised? They are carrying on Jesus' healing work.

crippled with arthritis are straightened up, those who are barren later give birth to babies, those bound by satanic powers through involvement with the occult are set free. It is not true that *all* who are sick are healed, but a good many are, either immediately or over a period of time during which there is persistent prayer and ministry . . .

Over the years I have seen a number of faith-healers at work, and most have left me troubled, if not disillusioned. The strong emotionalism of the meeting, the persuasive pleas for money, the unconfirmed claims of healing — all have left me wary and sceptical . . .

I had seen *some* healings — together with the striking effect of them — in my own ministry. But never before had I found such a wholesome and powerful healing ministry as at Yorba Linda. (*pp. 50-3*)

b When David Watson learned that he had cancer, three pastors (or ministers) from this church flew all the way from America to visit him in hospital in England.

But as we talked, they sensed the power of God coming upon them, so they began to pray. They praised God for his presence with us, for his authority over life and death, and they prayed against the spirit of unbelief, fear and death that was pervading the room.

After some time of praise and worship, Blaine became aware of the activity of the Holy Spirit, and laid hands on my abdomen. The three of them went on praying, cursing the cancer in the name of Christ, commanding it to wither, and then they claimed God's healing in my body . . .

I felt a tremendous surge of heat as well as vibrations in my body, and I knew that God was at work. This went on for half an hour or more, and we all had no doubt that God was with us . . .

As they left, I was undoubtedly 'doing' very well. I was bursting with praise. It was as though I had been lifted up into the presence of God, bathed in his glory and enveloped in his love. The light of Christ banished any remaining areas of doubt and fear, and I knew that, whatever the future might hold, I was safe in his hands. (*p. 56*)

c David Watson's cancer was diagnosed in January 1983 and he was given a year to live. Eleven months later he wrote:

The future officially is bleak, and I am getting used to people looking at me as a dying man under sentence of death. Nothing is certain. I'm not out of the wood yet. Everything is a matter of faith . . .

What we may not realise is how much we are trapped by our own thoughts and words. If we fill our minds with negative ideas, we may plunge into self-pity, despondency or fear. Even our bodies may react negatively with disease. The more we reflect on our hurts, the more we shall be bound by bitterness and prone to physical afflictions, such as arthritis . . .

I have had to watch all this carefully over the last eleven months. When I've had a difficult day or week, I sometimes find myself saying, especially in the middle of the night, 'I've got cancer, it's spreading and I'm dying. How am I going to tell the children?' At times like these I sweat a bit. But when I am more awake I realise that negative thoughts only accelerate the disease and

could lead to an early death . . .

In order to maintain a positive faith and not give way to negative fears, I have found it important to go on thanking God for the truth of his word and for the power of his Spirit at work within me. (*pp. 152–5*)

d David Watson finished writing this book in January 1984. In his last chapter, he wrote:

'God hasn't done anything for David,' people are now beginning to say. 'We've prayed and prayed, and nothing has happened at all.' Medically speaking, that seems to be true . . . However God has been far from inactive in my life . . . He showed me that all my preaching, writing and other ministry was absolutely *nothing* compared to my love-relationship with him. In fact, my sheer busyness had squeezed out the close intimacy I had known with him during the first few months of the year after my operation. (*pp. 170–1*)

Previously in the book, he had said:

Nothing is more important than our relationship with God, both for this life and for the next. (*p. 158*)

He finished the book with these words:

'Father, not my will but yours be done.' In that position of security I have experienced once again his perfect love, a love that casts out all fear.

David Watson died on 18 February 1984.

From a
1. *What do you think was most striking about the church called The Vineyard, from the description given here?*
2. *What criticisms are made of some faith healers?*

From b
3. *Describe how Christian healing was carried out on David Watson.*
4. *How did it make him feel?*

From c
5. *Do you think David Watson is right when he says that the state of our minds can affect our bodily health? Explain.*
6. *What evidence is there that David Watson was afraid that he would die of the cancer?*

From d
7. *In what sense was David Watson's death a failure?*
8. *What had his illness taught him about God?*

The lame can walk

Jesus' headquarters seem to have been at Capernaum, a little town on the shores of the Sea of Galilee. When the people heard that he was at home, they crowded around his house, and he preached to them. There was a small group of people particularly keen to see Jesus, but they could not get through the crowds to him. They were four people who had brought their paralysed friend on a stretcher. Not to be deterred, they climbed up onto the roof of

The ruins of Capernaum can still be seen today on the shores of the Sea of Galilee. The remains of an impressive synagogue stand out in the centre — but this one was built at least 150 years after Jesus' time.

Jesus' house and began to break up the roof until there was a hole large enough through which to lower their friend.

Jesus was impressed by such faith as this. He turned his attention to the paralysed man who now lay in front of him, on his stretcher. Going to the root of the man's trouble, Jesus said to him, 'Your sins are forgiven, my friend.' Now this might seem to us a strange thing for Jesus to say, but remember that many people in those days regarded illness as a punishment for their wrong doings. So Jesus was dealing with this man's troubled conscience and assuring him of God's forgiveness. This burden of guilt had to be lifted before any physical healing could take place.

The religious lawyers who were there objected to Jesus' claim to forgive sins. They thought it was blasphemy because they knew that only God could forgive sins. Jesus guessed what they were thinking and, to prove that he really was working by the power of God and that the man's sins had been forgiven, he told the man to get up, take his bed and go home. And he did just that. After all, anyone can go round making claims to forgive sins, but now Jesus had proved how special he was by making the lame man walk. The people were aware of God's power among them and they praised God for this wonderful miracle that they had witnessed. And, since the Pharisees believed that illness was the result of sin, they had to believe that the man's sins were forgiven when they saw him walk.

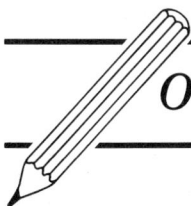

Over to you

1. If you want to read this story in the Bible, look it up in either Mark 2:1–12 or Luke 5:18–26.

2. In view of the type of houses inhabited by the ordinary people of Jesus' day (see section C), explain why it was easy for the friends to get onto the roof with a man on a stretcher, and to break it up.
3. How did Jesus know that this group of people had great faith in him?
4. Explain the connection seen between sin and suffering by Jews of Jesus' day.
5. Even today, people say, 'Why me?', 'What did she/he do to deserve this?' and 'Be sure your sins will find you out.' Why do they say these things? What do such sayings suggest about the reason for suffering?
6. Can you think of any bodily illnesses which are caused by a person's state of mind? (e.g. What can happen to someone in a state of shock? What are 'butterflies in the tummy'?)
7. Why did the lawyers take offence at Jesus in this incident?
8. Why do you think the Gospel writers included this story? (i.e. What were they trying to tell us about Jesus?)
9. Imagine that you are the man who was paralysed. Write out the conversation that took place between you and your wife when you arrived home carrying your bed.

C Housing

Poor people of Jesus' day had very small houses built of cheap materials which were readily available, like mud and straw bricks. They were box-shaped, at ground-floor level only, with thin, flat roofs which were probably made by laying branches across roughly cut wooden rafters and plastering the whole of it with mud. The roofs had parapets round them for safety and a staircase leading up to them on the outside of the house. The roof space was used as an extra living area in the hot weather and for such things as drying vegetables. Inside the house there was a raised section where the family slept at night, since their animals were given shelter at ground level. Nooks and crannies would be made around the walls for storage.

Houses like this can still be seen today in Mediterranean countries, in the poorer areas, often with large families living in them.

Lepers are made clean

One day, a man suffering from leprosy approached Jesus, flung himself at his feet and begged to be healed. The natural reaction for a Jew would have been to draw back from the leper because he was considered 'unclean'. Anyone who came into contact with such a person also became unclean and unable to take part in public religious ceremonies while in this state. Yet Jesus stretched out his hand and touched the man when he healed him.

Then Jesus sent him off to see a priest, as the Law demanded. He had to offer his sacrifices to God and get a clean bill of health from the priest so that he could return home to his family.

Jesus also commanded the man not to tell anyone about how he was cured. But he just could not keep it to himself, so the news of this miracle spread far and wide. Soon, many more sick people were clamouring to see Jesus.

Over to you

1. Read the story from Mark 1:40–5 or another Gospel.
2. Look up the passage from Leviticus which is quoted in section **D** and explain why the leprosy sufferer was breaking the Law to approach Jesus as he did.
3. How do we know that the leper had faith in Jesus?
4. Why was it so remarkable for Jesus to touch the leper? Why do you think he did it?
5. Look up Leviticus 14:4, 10 and 21–2 to find out what sacrifices were required of him. Either make a note of them or draw them.
6. Why do you think Jesus wanted secrecy?
7. What picture of Jesus comes across to you from this story? What was he like?
8. Imagine you are the man who was cured of leprosy by Jesus. Write a letter to a friend explaining how Jesus changed your life.

D Leprosy

Leprosy is rarely found in Western countries today but it is still a serious and quite common disease in countries of Africa and Asia. This is not because it is a tropical disease, but because Western countries have a better standard of hygiene.

Leprosy is caused by a bacillus that attacks the skin, nerves and muscles of the arms, legs and face. The first signs of it are white patches of skin which, when tested with a needle, have no feeling in them. These patches spread, making more and more of the skin insensitive. It is dangerous when leprosy sufferers lose all feeling in their hands and feet, especially in countries where people go barefoot and where cooking is done on open fires. There is the danger that they will tread on a thorn, badly stub their fingers or toes on hard objects, or scald, burn or cut themselves — all without realising it. These wounds could fester and result in open sores. Constant stubbing of the fingers and toes actually wears away the bones, leaving only stumps for hands and feet. So leprosy sufferers can become crippled. They can also become disfigured, especially when lumps grow on the face. Leprosy in itself is not a killer, but it can leave the sufferer weak and unable to resist other diseases which may kill.

Leprosy is not as highly contagious as many people think. Today, leprosy sufferers can be treated with drugs in their own homes. Leprosy can be cured as long as the disease is caught before it has crippled people. But because sufferers become so hideously deformed, this disease has always aroused repulsion and fear in other people. Leprosy sufferers have usually been driven away from their homes and forced to live away from human habitation, maybe with others in a leper colony. In Indian villages today, lepers are cast out and spoken of afterwards as if they had died.

In Jesus' day the Law, described in great detail in Leviticus 13 and 14, governed any spreading skin disease, including leprosy. It said that as soon as there was any sign of a skin complaint the sufferer should consult a priest. The priest would examine him and, if he was not sure about the diagnosis, he would keep the person in isolation and look at him after a week. If the skin complaint had not spread, he would keep him for a further week, as a double precaution and then examine him again and let him return home. However, if the priest considered it to be a serious skin disease, he would pronounce the person to be unclean. This meant that he could not come into contact with other people and could not attend religious services. Anyone who came in contact with him would also become 'unclean' and would have to be specially cleansed before being allowed to take part in religion. The Law stated:

A person who has a dreaded skin-disease must wear torn clothes, leave his hair uncombed, cover the lower part of his face, and call out, 'Unclean, unclean!' He remains unclean as long as he has the disease, and he must live outside the camp, away from others. (Leviticus 13:45—6)

People do recover from some skin diseases without treatment, including some forms of leprosy. Leviticus 14 gives instructions in that case. The priest would go out and examine the person to make sure that he was well before he came into contact with others. Then the person would have to bring animals and birds for the priest to sacrifice to God. This was to show that the cleansed person was sorry for his sins which were thought to have caused him to suffer from leprosy in the first place.

These leprosy sufferers are from the African country of Malawi. Notice the boy's feet and the man's disfigured face. Christian charities like The Leprosy Mission carry on Jesus' work today by trying to help and heal leprosy sufferers.

The deaf can hear

When Jesus was in Gentile territory, north of Galilee, some people brought him a deaf-mute to heal. Jesus took him aside by himself and showed the man by his actions that he was about to heal him. He put his fingers in the man's ears to show him that he would hear again and touched his tongue to show him that he would be able to talk. He used spittle, which was commonly regarded as a healing agent. All this was presumably so that the man could put his faith in Jesus. Then Jesus looked up to heaven, to show that he was calling on God's help, gave a deep groan, and said to the man 'Open up!' At this, the man was cured. He could hear and he began to talk without any trouble. Although Jesus asked for secrecy, the people just could not keep this to themselves. When others heard about it, they said with amazement:

'He even causes the deaf to hear and the dumb to speak!' (Mark 7:37)

The village of Bethany today, where Martha, Mary and Lazarus once lived.

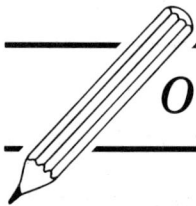

Over to you

1. Why is it very difficult for deaf people to speak properly, especially if they were born deaf?
2. One of the greatest problems for deaf people is that they look perfectly normal. Discuss why this should be a problem and any other difficulties that deaf people might have because of their handicap.
3. Work out a message in sign language to give to others in the class.
4. Have you any ideas why Jesus gave a deep groan while performing this miracle?
5. The people probably saw this miracle as a fulfilment of Old Testament prophecies about the Messiah. Look up the passages in section **A** on page 46 and write out the lines which came true in this incident.

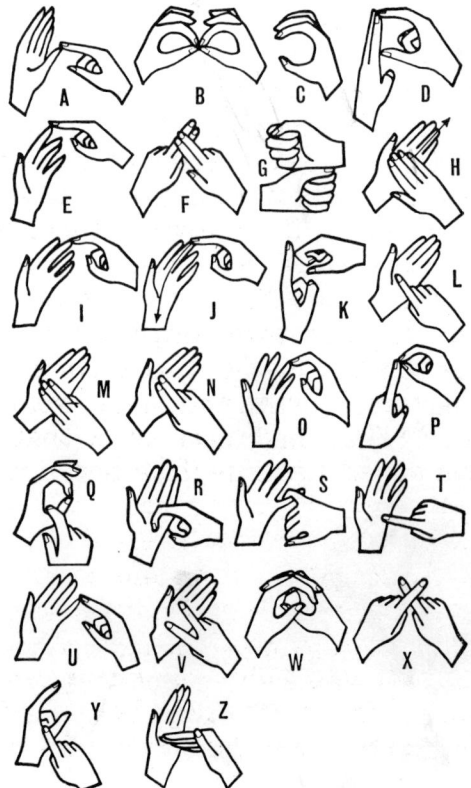

The dead are raised to life

God is recognised in Judaism and Christianity as the Creator who has authority over life and death. Therefore, for those who believe in God, the raising from the dead miracles are supreme examples of God's power working through Jesus.

Understandably there are only a few such miracles claimed for Jesus. Matthew, Mark and Luke all record the raising of Jairus' twelve-year-old daughter. She was said to be dead, and the people who had gathered at the house were already wailing loudly, as was their custom. Yet Jesus said: 'The child is not dead — she is only sleeping!' (Mark 5:39) This has led people to suggest that the girl was in a coma, from which Jesus roused her.

Luke's Gospel also records the raising to life of a widow's son. This took place at a town called Nain. Jesus came across a funeral procession to bury the only son of a widow. We are told that when Jesus saw the woman 'his heart was filled with pity for her' (Luke 7:13), for she now had no one to support her. He told her to stop crying and he halted the procession. Then Jesus ordered the young man to get up and, to everyone's amazement, he did.

John's Gospel records a different story: the raising of Lazarus. John used this story to help his readers think about the meaning of Jesus as the giver of life, and to prepare them for the story of Jesus' own resurrection. The story leaves us in no doubt that Lazarus was well and truly dead. He was three days buried by the time Jesus reached his home town of Bethany. Lazarus' sisters, Martha and Mary, went out to meet Jesus. They had been sure that Jesus could have saved Lazarus if he had arrived in time but all they could do now was to cling to the Jewish belief in the future day of resurrection. John saw that Jesus offered more than this belief in the Last Day. He knew that there was a quality of life which people can already experience here and now, and which cannot be threatened by the death of the body (elsewhere in this Gospel, he calls this 'Eternal Life'):

'Your brother will rise to life,' Jesus told her. 'I know,' she replied, 'that he will rise to life on the last day.' Jesus said to her, 'I am the resurrection and the life. Whoever believes in me will live, even though he dies; and whoever lives and believes in me will never die. Do you believe this?' 'Yes, Lord!' she answered. 'I do believe that you are the Messiah, the Son of God, who was to come into the world.' (John 11:23–7)

Jesus was so moved with compassion for the grieving sisters, who were his dear friends, that he wept with them. Some people asked why he had done nothing to save Lazarus from dying, but Jesus did more than this. He went over to the tomb, ordered the stone to be rolled away from the entrance, and he called for Lazarus. Lazarus came out, still wrapped up in his burial shroud.

Over to you

1. Why do people find the raising from death miracles most difficult to believe?
2. What methods do people use today to try to bring people out of comas?
3. Look up Luke 7:16–17. How did the onlookers respond to the raising of the dead man?
4. Copy out the 'I am' saying from the passage that is quoted.
5. Although in this story Lazarus' dead body was revived, 'eternal life' does not normally mean living for ever in a physical body on earth. If you think you know what it means, try to explain it.
6. Draw a picture of Lazarus coming out of the tomb.

E Exorcism

This is the word used to describe the casting out of evil spirits. In Jesus' day, demon-possession was a common explanation for illnesses which had no other obvious cause, like mental illnesses. Even though most people in the West no longer believe in demon-possession, people still say things like 'What's got into you today?' to someone who is acting out of character, and adults might say of a particularly naughty child, 'He's got the devil in him.'

Exorcism was thought of as a battle against the evil spirits inside a person. The exorcist had to act with great authority and gain power over the demons so that they obeyed him when he ordered them to leave the sick person.

The Jews thought of the coming of God's kingdom at the end of the world in terms of a battle between the forces of good and evil, between God and the Devil. Therefore Jesus'

Some Christians today still believe in demon-possession. In this photograph, a priest is performing an exorcism in a church in Britain.

exorcisms were seen by his followers as a sign that the Kingdom of God was being established:

'It is . . . by means of God's power that I drive out demons, and this proves that the Kingdom of God has already come to you.' (Luke 11:20)

The following example of one of Jesus' exorcisms shows the demon trying to gain the upper hand by naming Jesus, but Jesus was more powerful and managed to silence him:

Just then a man with an evil spirit in him came into the synagogue and screamed, 'What do you want with us, Jesus of Nazareth? Are you here to destroy us? I know who you are — you are God's holy messenger!' Jesus ordered the spirit, 'Be quiet, and come out of the man!' The evil spirit shook the man hard, gave a loud scream, and came out of him. The people were all so amazed that they started saying to one another, 'What is this? Is it some kind of new teaching? This man has authority to give orders to the evil spirits, and they obey him!' (Mark 1:23–7)

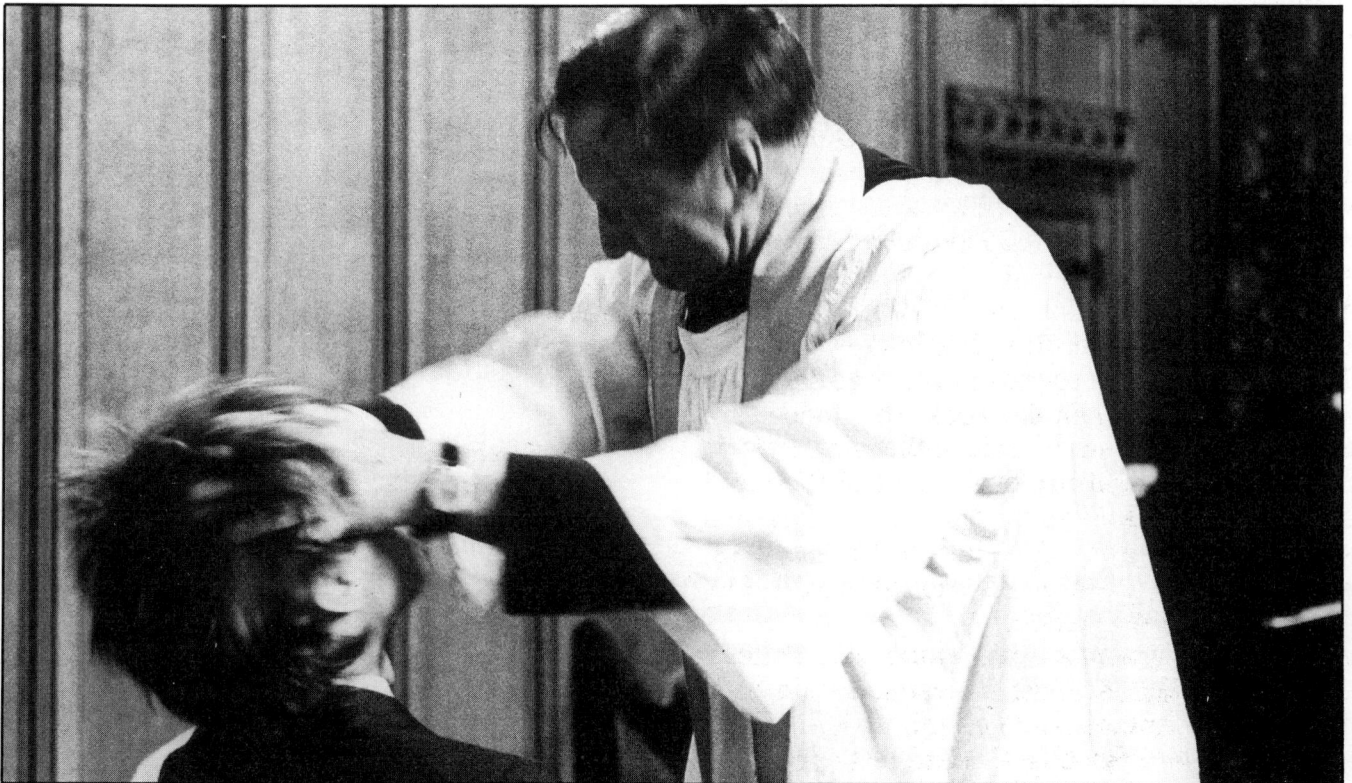

'Even the wind and the sea obey him'

There was one other type of miracle that the Gospel writers included: Jesus' power over natural things like the weather. These stories of his calming the storm on the Sea of Galilee, walking on the water and multiplying food to feed five thousand people are all very important. God was recognised as the Creator of the world and here was Jesus taking control over the forces of nature. So, like the raising from dead miracles, these too point to Jesus' divine power.

The Feeding of the Five Thousand is the only miracle recorded in all four Gospels (Mt 14:13; Mk 6:30; Lk 9:10; Jn 6:1) and there is also another version of it, the Feeding of the Four Thousand. Jesus went off with his disciples, to try to be alone with them for a while, but the crowds pursued him. We might have expected Jesus to be annoyed, but on this occasion Mark says:

> His heart was filled with pity for them, because they were like sheep without a shepherd. So he began to teach them many things. (Mark 6:34)

By the end of the day everyone was hungry, but they were far from home. The disciples suggested that Jesus send them all away to nearby farms and villages to buy food. Jesus had other ideas. You can imagine the disciples' surprise when he told them to feed the crowd themselves: they had only five loaves and two fish. Jesus told them to make everyone sit down in orderly rows. Then he took the food and, looking up to heaven, he said a blessing over it as is the Jewish custom, broke up the food and gave it to the disciples to distribute. The five thousand people or more all ate to their hearts' content; and there were still enough scraps left over to fill twelve baskets.

As a nature miracle, this alone would have been a sign of God's power in Jesus; but, in fact, this story is full of symbolism which points again and again to the Christian belief that Jesus was the Messiah:

This 4th–5th-century mosaic of the bread and fish comes from a church at Tabgha, on the shores of the Sea of Galilee — the traditional site of the feeding of the five thousand.

1 The setting is that of a great feast. The Jews sometimes pictured the Kingdom of God like this. The host of the banquet was God himself, or his representative, the Messiah. So this miracle presents Jesus as the Messiah, providing people with salvation.

2 Another Old Testament image of the Messiah was as a shepherd. This is how Jesus is portrayed here, caring for and guiding the people.

> And he shall stand and feed his flock
>   in the strength of the LORD.
> (Micah 5:4 *RSV*)

3 The actions of Jesus in blessing, breaking and giving the food remind Christian readers of Jesus' Last Supper and the Holy Communion service at church (see Section **F**). At the Last Supper Jesus did exactly the same with the bread, which represented his body. So this is a reminder of Jesus' death and resurrection: the core of the Gospel message. In church, the priest, acting like Jesus, does the same thing so that Christians continue to eat bread to represent Christ's presence with them. They do not eat enough to feed their bodies, instead it is a symbol that their souls are being fed. That is why John's Gospel speaks of Jesus himself as the Bread of Life (meaning eternal life).

4 Moses, perhaps the greatest of all the Jewish leaders, had also miraculously fed great crowds of people. When he was leading the People of God through the Wilderness he prayed to God for food, and God sent them manna to eat (a white, sticky substance found on plants early in the morning). So here we have a picture of Jesus as a New Moses.

5 The numbers in the story are there for a purpose. In the Old Testament we read of the *twelve* tribes of Israel; and the Old Testament starts with the *five* books of Moses, containing the laws of Israel. This is a way of saying that Jesus was starting a New Israel. Also the *five* loaves and *two* fish add up to *seven*, which was regarded as the perfect number in Judaism.

6 We know that the Jews of Jesus' day were looking out for their Messiah. Some people were actively preparing themselves to fight in the rebellion as soon as the Messiah appeared. Galilee in particular, safely tucked away in the north of the country, was a hot-house for such freedom fighters, called Zealots because of their zeal, or eagerness, to free Israel from the Romans. It could be that these five thousand men were gathered there in the hope that Jesus would lead them in such a rebellion. It is interesting that the story in John's Gospel ends with them wanting to make Jesus their 'king' (Messiah) by force. When Jesus realised this he made off into the hills by himself. This was not the sort of Messiah he intended to be.

Over to you

1. Write about a situation when you wanted to get on with something but were prevented from doing so, perhaps by a younger brother or sister. Try to express how you felt.
2. Explain why it was thought that nature miracles showed Jesus to have divine power (i.e. the power of God).
3. What other explanations could there be for this miracle apart from the multiplication of the bread and fish?
4. If the people had followed Jesus' example, and shared out what they had brought with them, could this be regarded as a miracle over *human* nature? Discuss this question in class.
5. Look up John 6:9 and make a note of the extra detail that John has in his version of the story.
6. Which of the six points, made about the symbols in the story, do you find most interesting? Explain why.
7. What image of salvation is used in Isaiah 25:6?
8. In one sentence, explain why the Gospel writers thought that it was important to record this miracle.

Art work

Choose one of the miracles which occur in Part 4 and illustrate it in some way on a piece of paper, for display.

Important words

Check the meaning of the following words by looking them up in the Word list at the back of this book. This is the order in which they occur in Part 4:

sign	unclean
miracle	exorcism
sacrifice	synagogue
demons	divine
demon-possession	Holy Communion
blasphemy	Zealot

Make sure you can spell
synagogue

F Background to the Holy Communion Service

This shows an open-air service of Holy Communion for Christians in India. The priest is in the centre. The wine is covered over, in a silver goblet (called a chalice) on the ground in front of him. (See also the photograph of Communion bread on p. 12.)

a A traditional Jewish grace:
Blessed art thou, Lord our God, King of the universe,
who bringest forth bread from the earth.

b Jesus, at the Feeding of the Five Thousand:
Then Jesus took the five loaves and the two fish, looked up to heaven, and gave thanks to God. He broke the loaves and gave them to his disciples to distribute to the people. (Mark 6:41)

c Jesus, at the Last Supper:
While they were eating, Jesus took a piece of bread, gave a prayer of thanks, broke it, and gave it to his disciples. 'Take it,' he said, 'this is my body.' (Mark 14:22)

Jesus also gave them wine to represent his blood.

d From one of the Holy Communion Services of the Church of England (omitting references to the wine — the Blood of Christ):

The priest prays:
Hear us, O Father,
through Christ thy Son our Lord; . . .
Who, in the same night that he was betrayed, took bread;
Here the priest takes the bread in his hands
and when he had given thanks to thee,
he broke it,
and gave it to his disciples, saying, Take, eat;
this is my body which is given for you:
do this in remembrance of me.

. . .

Later, the priest breaks the consecrated bread, saying:
We break this bread to share in the body of Christ.
Later, the priest gives each communicant a piece of bread, saying:
The body of our Lord Jesus Christ, which was given for you, preserve your body and soul unto everlasting life. Take and eat this in remembrance that Christ died for you, and feed on him in your heart by faith with thanksgiving.
(Author's words in italics)

A Sabbath miracle

It was the Sabbath day. Women had already finished their housework and prepared the best meal of the week, ready for the following day. Workmen had downed tools, had a good wash and put on their best clothes. The animals still had to be fed and watered, of course, but nothing was done which could possibly be left until the next day. Merchants could not carry their loads or travel any great distance on the Sabbath. The shops were closed and all was quiet. People took it easy on the Sabbath, spent time with their families, and many of them attended religious services. The Sabbath day was the Jewish holy day and a day of rest.

Jesus went along to his local synagogue to join with others in worshipping God and learning from the holy Scriptures. There was a man in the congregation who had a withered arm, and people wondered if Jesus would heal him. The Pharisees were especially interested to see what Jesus would do. They belonged to a religious party which was very concerned that the Jewish laws should be kept. They knew that it was against the law to heal anyone on the Sabbath, unless it was a matter of life or death. If Jesus healed this man, they could use it in evidence against him.

Jesus knew what they were thinking and he was both angry with the Pharisees and sorry for them. They had become so bound up with the laws that they did not seem to have any pity for the man who was suffering. Jesus called the man out in front of them all. Then he asked out loud:

'What does our Law allow us to do on the Sabbath? To help or to harm? To save a man's life or to destroy it?' (Mark 3:4)

Jesus wanted them to see the positive value of the Sabbath law, not just the negative side which said 'Don't do this...', 'Don't do that...'. Jesus put his question in such a way that no one answered him. They would not want to say that the Sabbath was for doing evil and for killing, but if they said it was for doing good and saving life, they would be encouraging Jesus to heal on the Sabbath, which was forbidden. Jesus went ahead anyway. He told the man to stretch out his arm. He obeyed Jesus and found that he was better. The Pharisees had been beaten. When they left the synagogue they plotted to do away with Jesus.

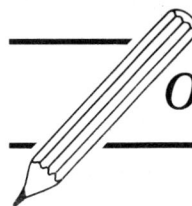

Over to you

1. How can you tell, from the beginning of this story, that Jesus was keeping the Sabbath as a holy day?
2. How do you think the man with the withered arm (and his family if he had one) would have suffered because of his disability?
3. Why do you think Jesus added 'To save a man's life or to destroy it?' Was he just exaggerating?
4. Copy out what Jesus said about the Sabbath law in Mark 2:27–8:
   a) What does Jesus consider to be more important: people or the law?
   b) Why is Jesus considered to have special authority over the Sabbath laws (assuming that he is speaking of himself in verse 28)?
5. Imagine that you were one of the Pharisees in the synagogue at the time of this incident. Write a report on it to send to the leading Pharisees in Jerusalem.
6. Can you think of any situations today where you might consider that it is right to break the law?
7. Remembering that the Sabbath was a holy day and a day of rest, can you see where 'holidays' have come from?

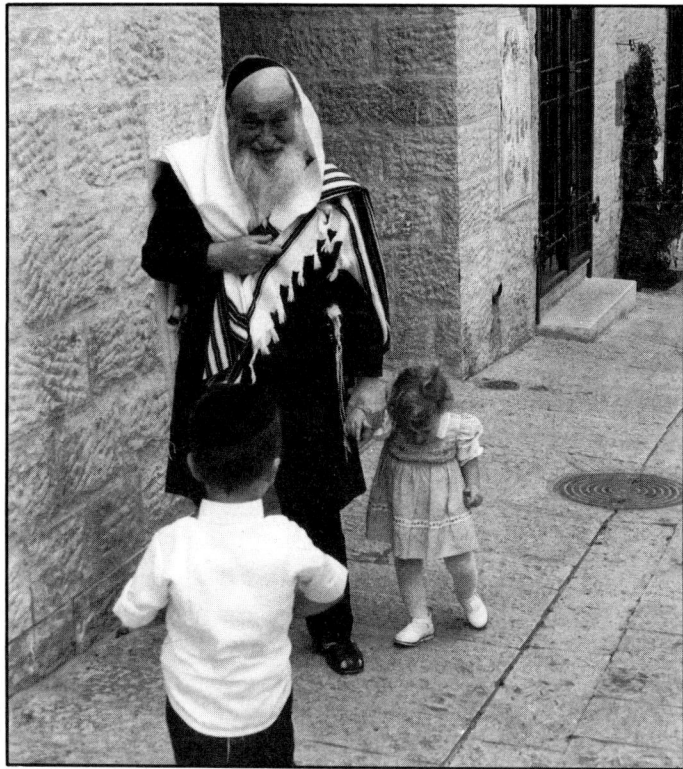

This was taken on a Sabbath day in Jerusalem — a time for the family to be together. The man has on his prayer shawl, ready to go to synagogue for the main service of the week.

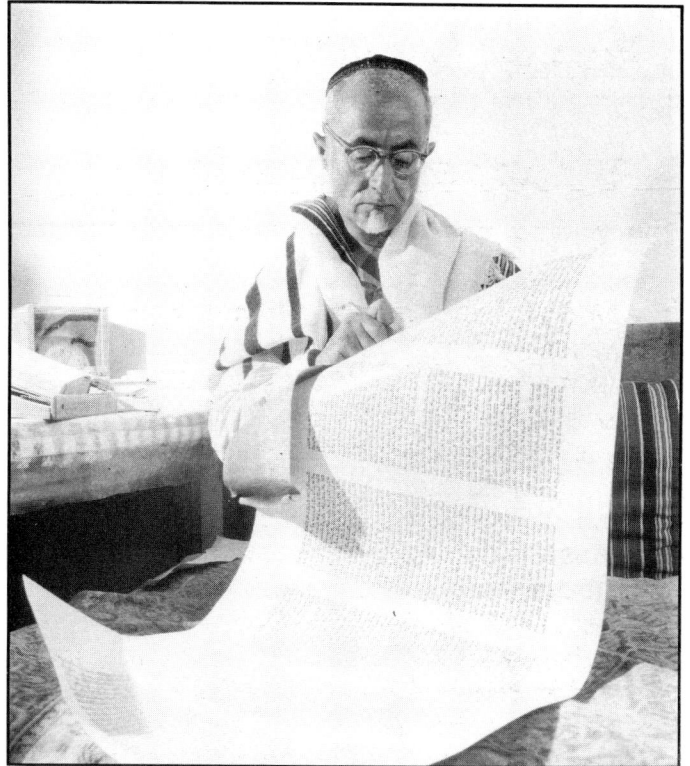

The Jewish laws are based on the first five books of the Bible, which Jews call the Torah ('teaching'). Torah scrolls are hand-written by scribes for use in the synagogues. Here is a scribe in Israel today, working on a Torah scroll.

A   *The Sabbath law*

'Observe the Sabbath and keep it holy. You have six days in which to do your work, but the seventh day is a day of rest dedicated to me. On that day no one is to work — neither you, your children, your slaves, your animals, nor the foreigners who live in your country. In six days I, the LORD, made the earth, the sky, the sea, and everything in them, but on the seventh day I rested. That is why I, the LORD, blessed the Sabbath and made it holy.'
(Exodus 20:8–11)

Quoted above is the fourth of the Ten Commandments from which the Sabbath law came. The word *sabbath* means to 'break off' or 'cease' from work. No unnecessary work is permitted on the Sabbath day. It is a holy day for worshipping God and studying the Scriptures. It is also a time for eating and relaxing with the family, celebrating the good things in life that God has created. The Sabbath is the seventh day of the Jewish week. Jewish days begin at sunset and not at midnight, so the Sabbath is equivalent to our Friday evening to Saturday night.

There are a number of incidents in the Gospels where Jesus was blamed for breaking the Sabbath law:

★ He let his disciples pick some corn and prepare it for eating (Mt 12:1; Mk 2:23; Lk 6:1).
★ He healed a man with a withered arm (Mt 12:9; Mk 3:1; Lk 6:6).
★ He healed a woman who was bent double (Lk 13:10).
★ He healed a man suffering from dropsy (Lk 14:1).
★ He healed a crippled man (Jn 5:1).
★ He healed a blind man (Jn 9:1).

B Synagogues

The word *synagogue* means 'assembly' or 'meeting'. It came to refer to the places where Jews met together for religious services and also for religious education and social gatherings.

The idea of meeting together in this way probably goes back to the sixth century BC when the Temple was destroyed and the Jews were taken into exile in a foreign land. They kept their religion alive by meeting together to worship God and study their Scriptures. We have no evidence of special buildings called synagogues before the second century BC.

In Jesus' day the synagogues were especially important for Jews like him who lived away from Jerusalem and were therefore some distance from the Temple. The synagogues were run by the Pharisees who chose readers and a preacher at each service from among the adult, male Jews who were present (there had to be at least ten of them there before the service could begin). The service consisted of prayers, psalms, readings from Scripture and a sermon.

Synagogues are the only places of worship for Jews today, since their Temple was destroyed in AD 70.

1. The Holy Ark – a cupboard for the Scrolls of the Law (the first five books of the Bible).

2. The bimah – a raised platform with a desk from which the scrolls are read. In Jesus' day it would also have had a seat from which the preacher gave his sermon. Today there is usually a small pulpit at the front of the synagogue.

3. Seats for the men – on the ground floor. In Jesus' day the seats probably ran along the walls, leaving more space for people to gather.

4. The balcony for the women and children. They were separated from the men.

C Religious groups in Jesus' day

The Pharisees

Any Jew could be a Pharisee. They were a religious party which began in the second century BC. Their name probably meant 'separated' because they stressed the differences between themselves and the Gentiles, and even perhaps the less religious Jews. They tried to keep strictly to the Jewish Law, discussing the meaning of the laws for their own day. They tended to take leading parts in running the synagogues, where they worshipped regularly.

The teachers of the Law

These may also be referred to in the Gospels as scribes, doctors of the law, lawyers, or rabbis. (The word *rabbi* means 'my teacher' and is used today as the title for Jewish religious leaders.) They are first heard of in the sixth century BC, when they helped the priests by writing up the records of the Jewish people in their Scriptures. Because of their knowledge of the Scriptures, particularly the Law books, they became teachers of Judaism and interpreted the Law for people. Many of them belonged to the Pharisee party.

The Sadducees

These were the old noble families. They were old-fashioned in their religion, keeping the Jewish laws which were written down in the Scriptures, but refusing to accept any new interpretations of the laws or any new religious beliefs. From them came the priests who ran the Temple in Jerusalem. So their main concern was with the Temple services and the sacrifices offered there. The High Priest was the most powerful Jewish religious leader. He was chosen by Rome and presided over the Sanhedrin, the Jewish court of seventy-one members consisting of both Sadducees and Pharisees.

There are no longer any priests in Judaism; the rabbis are the religious leaders today. This rabbi, in a British synagogue, is reading the Law from the Torah scroll.

Tax collectors and sinners

Another reason why many of the Pharisees disapproved of Jesus was that he kept company with people whom they thought no self-respecting rabbi would be seen dead with. Jesus was not concerned about his own reputation, but helped those who needed him most. So he mixed with sinners, those people who did not try to keep all the religious laws. He ate with tax collectors, who were disliked. He talked with women, whose modesty should have kept them at a safe distance. He took notice of children, whom other adults ignored. He touched lepers and others who were considered 'unclean'. His reply to the Pharisees was that healthy people do not need a doctor, only the sick. Jesus was exasperated with these Pharisees. It seemed that nothing would satisfy them. They had criticised John the Baptist for being too strict about his religion, and now they criticised him for going the other way and called him 'a glutton and a drinker, a friend of tax collectors and other outcasts!' (Luke 7:34)

One day Jesus was passing through Jericho, the home of Zacchaeus, a wealthy taxman. So keen was Zacchaeus to catch a glimpse of Jesus that he took up an undignified position in one of the sycamore trees that lined the narrow road. When Jesus came along, he stopped beneath that very tree and invited himself to Zacchaeus' house. Zacchaeus climbed down as fast as he could and gladly agreed.

There was a general murmur of disapproval. Why was Jesus bothering with his sort? No one likes tax collectors at the best of times, and these Jewish tax collectors were mostly swindlers. What is more, they were taking money from their own people to give to the hated Romans. Under the Roman Empire there was a system of farming out the taxes. Each tax area was put up to tender. Whoever bid the highest for it got the job. That tax collector, or firm of tax collectors, then had to make sure the people paid enough taxes to pay off the bill to Rome as well as providing the taxman's wages. Who was to say what a fair wage would be? The system encouraged greed, and most tax collec-tors were out for all they could get.

Zacchaeus was so overwhelmed by Jesus' generous behaviour towards him that he became a changed man. He said that he would give away half of his possessions to charity and he would repay the debt four times over in any known cases where he had cheated someone. This was much more than the law required. Jesus had brought Zacchaeus salvation, for Zacchaeus had repented of his sins and made up for them.

Over to you

1. What did Jesus mean by the saying, 'People who are well do not need a doctor, but only those who are sick', when speaking of his care for the out-casts? If you do not know the answer, it may help to look up the full passage in Mark 2:15–17 or Luke 5:29–32.

2. What sort of people in our society might be considered unsuitable for respectable people to mix with?

3. Draw a picture-strip, showing each stage of the story of Zacchaeus. (You may want to look it up in Luke 19:1—10.)

4. Look up Luke 19:10. There we see that the story was used to show Jesus as the saviour of sinners. Copy out the saying about Jesus that speaks of the Son of Man.

5. Look up the Parable of the Pharisee and the Tax Collector in Luke 18:9—14. Jesus told this story to 'people who were sure of their own goodness and despised everybody else'. Describe in your own words what the Pharisee was like in this story and what the tax collector was like or act out the scene in small groups. Jesus has exaggerated the contrast between the two in order to make his point.

The Salvation Army

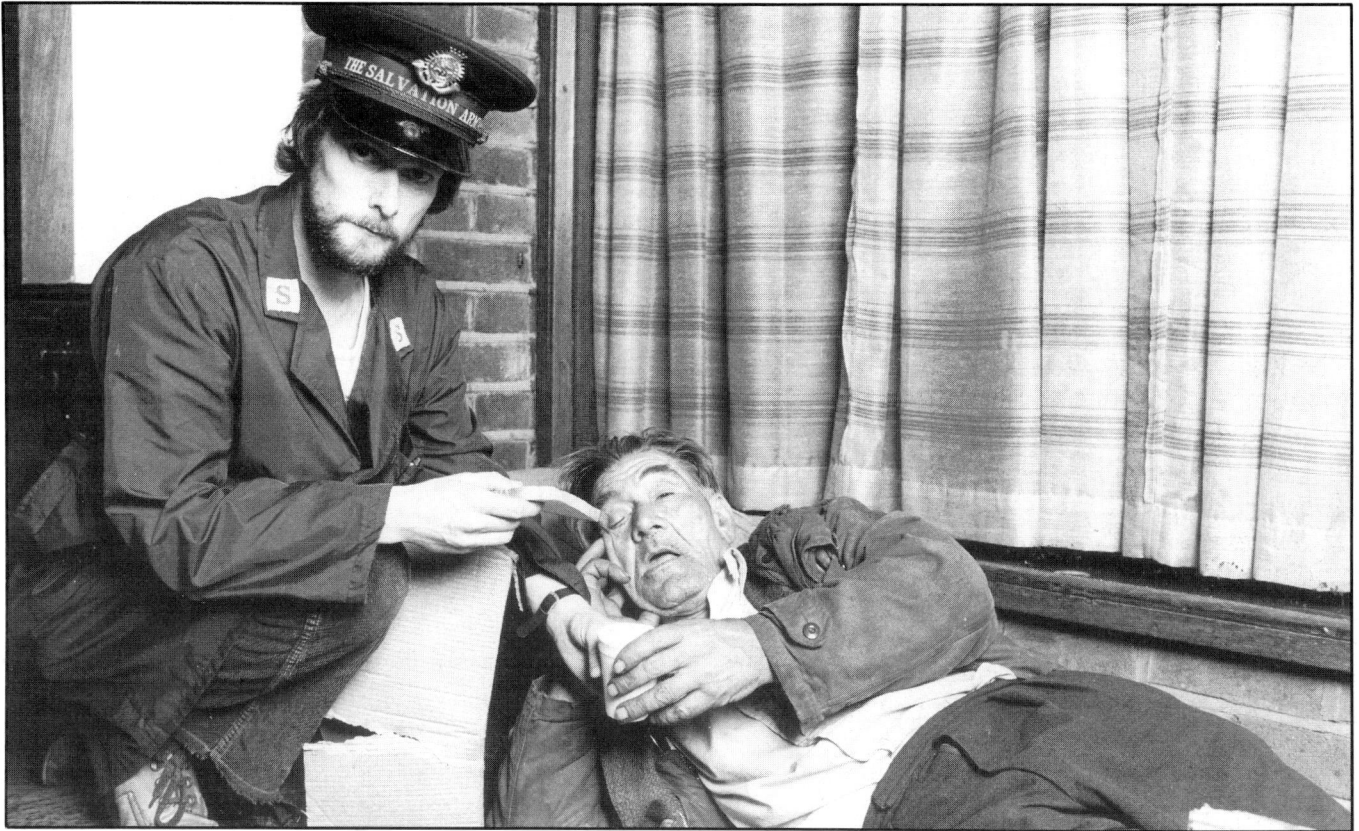

The Salvation Army is well known for its work among the single homeless. This officer is giving bread and soup to a man who is sleeping rough.

The Salvation Army is a church which grew up in the nineteenth century out of a Christian concern for the down-and-outs in our society. William Booth (1829–1912) was a preacher who worked in the poor East End of London. He saw drunkenness, poverty and squalor all around him. Following Jesus' example, he preached about God's love, out on the streets, to the disreputable people who were unlikely to come to church. He made people feel that God cared about them, whoever they were.

William Booth also believed that people could not listen to the Gospel with cold feet and empty stomachs. He and his followers declared war on poverty. They set about helping the needy people they came across: starving families, homeless men and women who slept out at night, prostitutes, criminals, drug addicts and drunkards, the sick and the mentally ill.

Booth wanted his church to be as efficient as a well-run army. It was an army which fought against evils and brought people love and hope. So it was called the Salvation Army. Today this church works throughout the world. It runs soup-kitchens and hostels for the homeless, it works with teenagers and the elderly, in hospitals and prisons, in factories and in schemes for the unemployed. The Salvation Army has church buildings called citadels, but its members also go out onto the streets to hold services, and regularly visit public houses to sell their newspapers. Salvationists are still not ashamed to show God's love to the sort of people whom others despise. They march in the footsteps of their founder, William Booth, who said in his last speech: 'While women weep, as they do now, I'll fight. While little children go hungry, as they do now, I'll fight. While men go to prison, in and out, I'll fight. While there yet remains one dark soul without the light of God, I'll fight.'

By what authority?

Jesus was approaching Jerusalem, the Holy City. From the little villages of Bethphage and Bethany, a few miles away, he made plans to enter the city in a particular way. He would ride in on a donkey. The Gospel writers could hardly avoid seeing the fulfilment of a prophecy by Zechariah:

> Rejoice, rejoice, people of Zion!
> Shout for joy, you people of Jerusalem!
> Look, your king is coming to you!

How can you tell that this is a Palm Sunday procession? These French pilgrims are following the traditional route that Jesus took, from Bethphage to the Old City of Jerusalem.

He comes triumphant and victorious,
> but humble and riding on a donkey —
> on a colt, the foal of a donkey.
(Zechariah 9:9)

Matthew quotes this prophecy and includes both the donkey and its foal in his story.

In this symbolic act, Jesus was proclaiming himself to be the Messiah. Many people recognised this and, waving palm branches and carpeting the road with their cloaks, they chanted:

'Praise God! God bless him who comes in the name of the Lord! God bless the King of Israel!' (John 12:13)

The Pharisees resented Jesus' popularity, but there was nothing they could do.

Jesus' followers were not surprised when he headed straight for the Temple. This was the heart of the Jewish faith and where the Messiah was expected to declare himself. On that occasion he merely surveyed the scene and withdrew. No doubt the soldiers were waiting for trouble. The next day, he returned to the Temple and this time he showed his authority. But instead of raising the flag for Judaism and rallying the Jewish forces, he began to clear out the Temple. He upset the stalls in the outer courtyard of those who sold birds and animals for sacrifice at exorbitant prices. He overturned the stalls of those who exchanged the pilgrims' money into Temple coinage at a handsome profit. He would not let people use the Temple courtyard as a short cut to the other side of the city, for this disturbed those who came there to worship. He taught them:

'It is written in the Scriptures that God said, "My Temple will be called a house of prayer for the people of all nations." But you have turned it into a hideout for thieves!' (Mark 11:17)

People of *all* nations? Jesus was only too well aware that there was a notice over the entrance to the inner courts of the Temple forbidding any Gentile to enter, on pain of death.

This 'cleansing of the Temple' was yet another, far more serious, reason for the religious leaders to oppose Jesus. Now the priests of Jerusalem, the Sadducees, joined with the Pharisees against him. They saw his behaviour in the Temple as verging on blasphemy. Who was this man to act as though he had God's authority? This was an insult to God himself!

When they confronted Jesus about this, and asked him by what authority he did these things, he would only ask them a question in return. He wanted to know if they thought John the Baptist had acted on God's authority. They were caught! If they said he had, then they ought to accept Jesus whom John baptized. On the other hand, so many people had accepted John as a prophet, that they dared not deny that God had inspired him. They said they did not know; so Jesus said that he would not answer either.

People still use the narrow road between Bethany and Bethphage. This is the road Jesus would have taken to Jerusalem, during his last Passover.

Over to you

1. a) What type of Messiah did Jesus represent by riding into Jerusalem on a donkey?
   b) In contrast, what would it have symbolised if Jesus had ridden in on a war-horse?
2. Why was Matthew so concerned to include the foal as well as the donkey in his account?
3. What Messianic title was used by the crowds who followed Jesus into Jerusalem?
4. Why did Jesus refer to the Temple as 'a hideout for thieves'?
5. Look up the diagram of the Temple on page 9. What were the three inner courts called, which were surrounded by the Court of Gentiles?
6. Write a report on Jesus' entry into Jerusalem and the scene in the Temple as if it were for a local Jewish newspaper at the time.
7. Do you think tourists should be encouraged into churches, or should such places be kept for people who want to worship? What do you think about the sale of souvenirs in cathedrals and entrance fees being charged for those who want to look around?

The final conflict

The walled city of Jerusalem was filled to the brim with visitors at that time of year. They packed the narrow streets, to the delight of the tradesmen, and poured into the Temple area. It was nearly the festival of Passover, the most important of the three pilgrim feasts, which Jews liked to celebrate in the Holy City. Each family offered its lamb for sacrifice at the Temple, before enjoying the roast meat at the big supper which started Passover week.

When there was no room left to stay in Jerusalem, pilgrims lodged by night in the surrounding villages. Jesus had friends in Bethany, and that is where he and his disciples stayed. They walked each day into the city, where Jesus taught the crowds in the Temple.

When Jesus was at the house of a man called Simon, in Bethany, a woman came in with an expensive bottle of perfume and poured it all over Jesus' head. There were those who criticised such waste when there were so many poor people around, but Jesus defended her. It was a pure act of love on her part. More than this,

Gethsemane means 'olive press'. This type was in use at the time of Jesus. The olives were put in the shallow basin and crushed by the stone being rolled over them. The oil was drained off. What do you think was put through the hole in the round stone, to move it?

Jesus pronounced that she was anointing his body beforehand for burial. He must have been aware of the danger of his position by then. He had already upset the Jewish authorities and, by continuing to preach in the Temple, he was putting his head further into the noose. In the event, Jesus' body was indeed buried in such haste, before the Sabbath began on Friday evening, that there was no time for the usual washing and anointing of his corpse.

According to the first three Gospels, Passover that year began on a Thursday evening. Jesus arranged to eat the Passover Supper in Jerusalem with his disciples and this is now known as the Last Supper because it was the last time that Jesus ate with his disciples before his death. At that meal, he took ordinary bread and wine and gave them a new meaning. The bread was to represent his body, and the wine his blood. He was leaving behind something solid to remember him by. Ever since then, most Christians have regularly held a service (called by various names, such as Holy Communion, the Eucharist, Mass, the Lord's Supper) in which they eat a small piece of bread and sometimes drink a sip of wine. They do this to remember Jesus' death and to represent their belief that he rose again and continues to be with them (see section F, p. 59).

After supper they left the city and took a short walk to the Garden of Gethsemane on the Mount of Olives. There Jesus prayed in earnest, for he knew that he did not have much time left. Like any of us, he was afraid to die, but in the end he was willing to do whatever God required of him:

'Not my will, however, but your will be done.'
(Luke 22:42)

It was there that Jesus was arrested, secretly for fear of the crowds, and taken away for trial.

So far, Jesus had acted with great authority and been recognised as the Messiah by others, but he had never publicly and plainly said that he was the Messiah. It was not until he was

This shows the Garden of Gethsemane on the Mount of Olives (you can see some olive trees in the foreground). At the back you can see the roof of the Church of All Nations, built over the traditional site where Jesus prayed.

taken before the Jewish court that he made this claim. After a number of attempts to convict him, the High Priest asked:

'Are you the Messiah, the Son of the Blessed God?'

Jesus said:

'I am.' (Mark 14:61–2)

This was enough for the Jews to condemn him. The High Priest tore his robes to express his shame that an imposter should make such a bold claim. Jesus was convicted of blasphemy.

If Jesus had been a political Messiah, then the triumphal entry into Jerusalem would have been the best opportunity to rally his supporters, establish himself in the Temple, and start the revolution. We have seen that this is not what Jesus did. He rode into the Holy City not on a war-horse but on a donkey, a sign of peace and humility. He did not attack Rome, but Judaism. Yet he was executed by the Romans as a rebel, which was an embarrassment to Christians and needed to be explained

if Christianity was not to be seen as a threat to Rome.

John tells us that the Jewish authorities did not have the right to execute Jesus themselves. This sounds likely, especially with Pontius Pilate, the Roman governor, in residence in Jerusalem at the time. Perhaps also they were afraid of his popularity with the common people and were not prepared to take the blame. The next morning, Friday, they handed him over to Pilate on the charge of claiming to be the king of the Jews. For a Roman, this would have been understood in a purely political way. Here was some rabble-rouser claiming authority, when it was the Romans who had authority over the Jews. The inscription on Jesus' cross read: 'The king of the Jews'. Christians believe that this was true — in a way — not that Jesus was a rebel leader, but that he was the true Messiah.

69

1. Why do you think Jesus is called 'the Lamb of God'? (John 1:29 and 36)
2. Look up the story of Jesus' anointing in Bethany in Mark 14:3–9 and try to draw a picture of the scene, showing the reactions of the different people there.
3. In view of the fact of the terrible poverty in many parts of the world today, do you think it is ever right to squander money? Consider the expense, luxury and excess of religious festivals like Christmas.
4. What other meaning might we see in Jesus' anointing at Bethany, as he approached his death? Remember who 'the anointed one' was.
5. What meaning did Jesus give to the bread and wine at the Last Supper?
6. When else had Jesus committed blasphemy in the eyes of the Jews? (See pages 51 and 67.)

Art work

Do an illustration for display of one of the ways mentioned in Part 5 in which Jesus offended the religious leaders (e.g. breaking the Sabbath law; mixing with disreputable people like Zacchaeus; winning over the common people — as shown in the triumphal entry into Jerusalem; and ordering people about in the Temple).

Important words

Check the meaning of the following words by looking them up in the Word list at the back of this book. This is the order in which they occur in Part 5:

Sabbath	Sadducee
Pharisee	Passover

Make sure you can spell
these four words (check where they have double letters)

E Passover

Lettuce
Charoset
Lamb bone
Roasted egg
Parsley
Horseradish

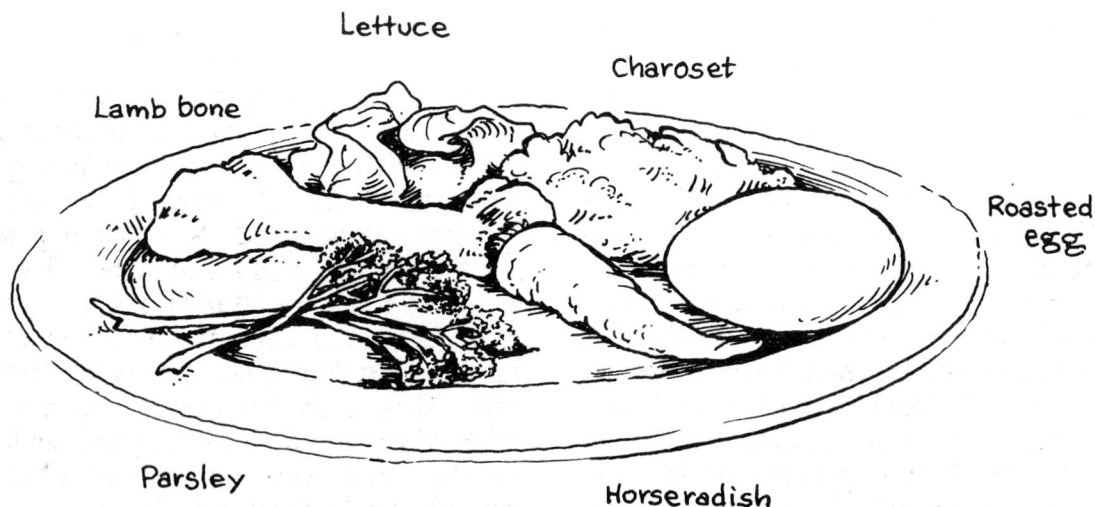

This is the most important of the annual Jewish festivals. It is a celebration of freedom: a time to remember that God takes particular care of his Chosen People, the Jews, and frees them from their enemies.

The Passover season comes in Spring and lasts a week. It starts with a special commemorative meal eaten on the first evening.

The story that is recalled at this supper is the Exodus, when they escaped from Egypt, possibly in about 1250 BC. They remember the terrible suffering of their ancestors in Egypt and how God appointed Moses to lead them to freedom:

God spoke to Moses and said 'I am the LORD . . .

So tell the Israelites that I say to them, "I am the LORD; I will rescue you and set you free from your slavery to the Egyptians. I will raise my mighty arm to bring terrible punishment upon them, and I will save you. I will make you my own people, and I will be your God. You will know that I am the LORD your God when I set you free from slavery in Egypt."' (Exodus 6:2, 6–7)

The story is retold by means of special symbolic foods:

★ **Lettuce** tastes nice at first, but can leave a bitter taste at the back of the mouth. This represents the fact that originally the Jews were happy to settle in Egypt until they were enslaved by the Pharaoh.

★ **Horseradish** is a very bitter root vegetable. It symbolises their bitter suffering as slaves.

★ **Charoset** is a mixture of mainly stewed apple and nuts. It looks a bit like cement and reminds the Jews that they were forced to work on the Pharaoh's building projects.

★ **Parsley** is dipped in **salt water** before they eat it. This stands for the small amount of food they had to survive on and their tears of misery.

★ **Unleavened bread** is like large, flat water-biscuits. They are eaten throughout Passover week (no other bread is allowed). It reminds them of the night the Jews escaped from Egypt in such a hurry that there was no time to wait for the dough to rise.

★ The **bone** is usually a lamb bone. It reminds them that Moses gave instructions for each family to kill and roast a lamb so that they would have a good meal inside them for the long journey ahead. The blood of the lamb was painted on their door-frames so that the angel of death would 'pass over' them that night and only punish the Egyptian households. This is where the festival gets its name. In Jesus' day, when the Temple still stood, lambs were sacrificed there in the afternoon, to be eaten at the Passover supper that evening.

★ The **egg** is roasted to symbolise the 'burnt offering' — another sacrifice which was made in the Temple at Passover.

This Passover supper is a big family occa-

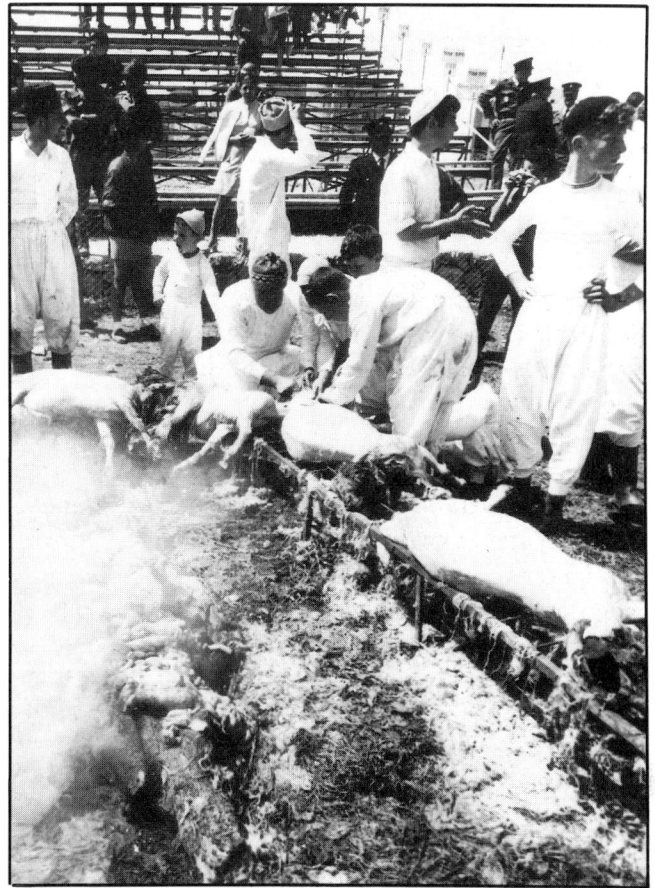

The Samaritans in Israel still sacrifice lambs to be roasted for Passover, as all the Jews did in Jesus' day.

sion, usually with many people gathered round the table. There is a festive atmosphere, with candles burning and plenty of wine to drink. A special feature of the Passover supper table is that a place is set for Elijah and a glass of wine filled for him. The Jews believe that this great prophet of old will return before their Messiah comes. Having thanked God for saving them in the past, they pray for Jews who are still oppressed today and look forward, at Passover, to the great time of salvation that they believe the Messiah will bring.

1. Read about the Exodus and the Passover in Exodus 12:1–17.
2. What special meals do you have to commemorate annual events?
3. What American festival is most like the Passover in that it celebrates the gaining of a people's freedom?

71

Part 6 The Christmas stories

Introduction

The Gospel writers were convinced that Jesus was the Messiah, but at what point did he *become* the Messiah? It seems that, at first, his baptism was understood to be the moment when the Holy Spirit came upon him, as if God was adopting him then as his son, the Messiah. When we look at the sermons of the early Christians, in the Book of Acts, we see that the 'good news' of salvation which was preached, before the Gospels were written, began with John the Baptist. This is from one of Peter's sermons:

'You know the message he [God] sent to the people of Israel, proclaiming the Good News of peace through Jesus Christ, who is Lord of all. You know of the great event that took place throughout the land of Israel, *beginning in Galilee after John preached his message of baptism.* You know about Jesus of Nazareth and how God poured out on him the Holy Spirit and power.' (Acts 10:36—8, author's italics)

Mark's Gospel also opens at this point in the story, and many scholars think that the first draft of John's Gospel may have started in this way too.

The Gospels of Matthew and Luke go back earlier than this and start with the birth of Jesus. Stories of Jesus' birth and childhood are found nowhere else in the New Testament. Another interesting fact to notice is that the Christmas stories in Matthew and Luke are different. In Matthew's Gospel we find the story of the wise men led by a star; in Luke's Gospel we read of Jesus being born in a stable and of angels appearing to some shepherds.

Why did these writers include the Christmas stories? It is not unusual for stories like these to grow up around a great person. There are similar stories connected with the birth of the Buddha, Muhammad and Guru Nanak, all great leaders of other religions. The basic historical facts may be embroidered, but the stories show how important that person was.

The birth stories recorded by Matthew and Luke tell of messages from God by angels and in dreams, of miraculous births (that of John the Baptist as well as of Jesus) and the guidance of a star. All these things were symbols which came from the Old Testament. When we explore their background, we can begin to

The story of Jesus' birth is the Gospel reading at this Christmas service in an Ethiopian church.

see the depth of meaning in these stories. The Gospel writers were not so much concerned with when, where and how Jesus was born, as with *why* God sent him and *who* he was. These stories convey the same good news as the rest of the material in the Gospels — that Jesus was the Messiah. But they show that Jesus was special from the moment of his conception; that God was in it from his beginning. Because these writers believed that Jesus was the Messiah, their living Lord and Saviour, they saw his birth as the most momentous event in history, when God began to bring about the salvation of the world. They have recorded their Christmas stories as powerful expressions of this belief.

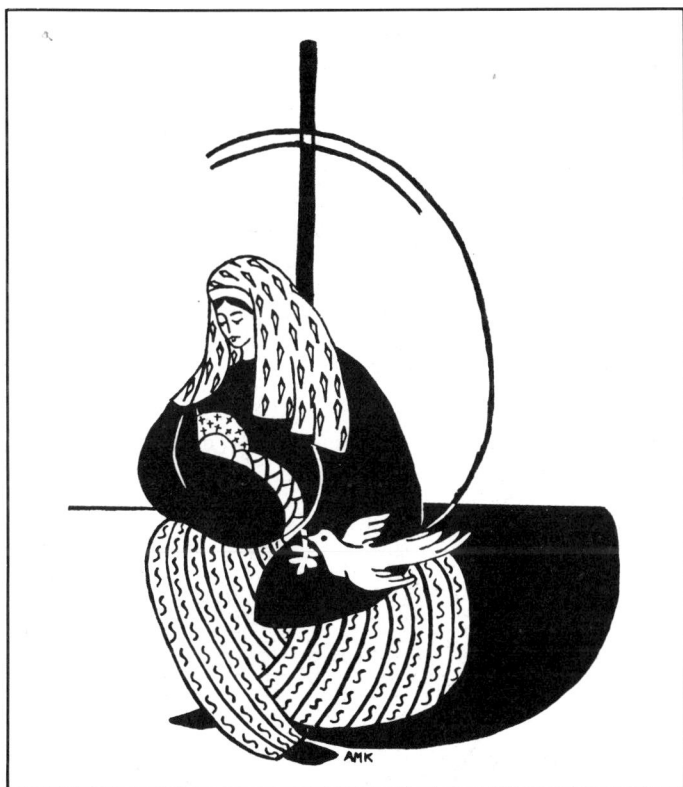

Like the Gospel writers, the artist who designed this Christmas card is also concerned with who Jesus was and why God sent him. She says: 'Jesus' birth cannot be separated from his death. The linking symbol is the dove which represents the Holy Spirit of God. Its tail encircles Mary and Jesus to form a cross as it passes through the wooden post in the background.'

This is a traditional symbol (right), made for a Christingle service when Jesus is celebrated as the Light of the World.

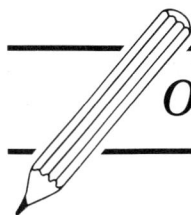

Over to you

1. In the sermon quoted above from the Book of Acts, where did the Christians begin their story of Jesus?
2. Where does Mark's Gospel begin the story of Jesus? (See Mark 1:2–8)
3. Which Gospels do *not* record stories of Jesus' birth?
4. Sort through some old Christmas cards, if you have any, and try to find one that illustrates the story from Matthew's Gospel, another to illustrate Luke's version, and one which puts the stories together. Fix these into your book and label them, saying which Gospels they illustrate.
5. Choose the best ending to complete the following sentence, and write it out in full in your book: *Birth stories like these grow up around great people*
   a) because we all like to hear about babies and children
   b) because they must have had miraculous births in order to grow up into such wonderful people
   c) to emphasise their importance.
6. The Christmas stories are saying that Jesus was sent into the world as the Messiah i.e. the Saviour, to bring people back to God. Design your own Christmas card showing how *you* would put across this message.

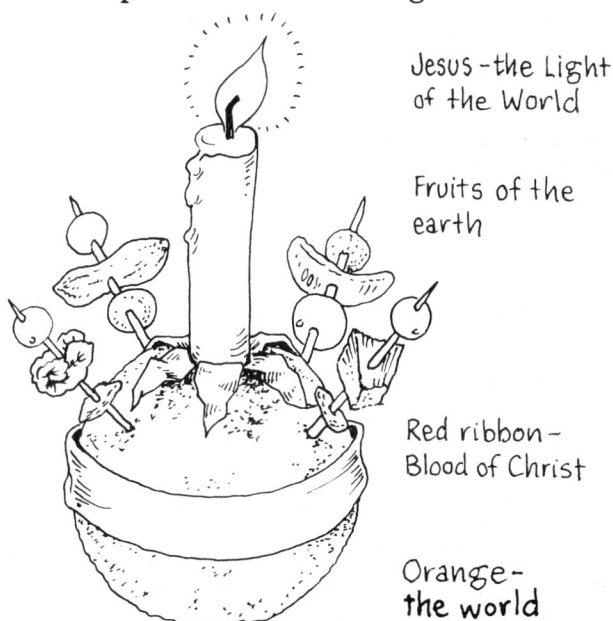

Jesus – the Light of the World

Fruits of the earth

Red ribbon – Blood of Christ

Orange – the world

A The Prologue of John's Gospel

[1] Before the world was created, the Word already existed; he was with God, and he was the same as God. [2] From the very beginning the Word was with God. [3] Through him God made all things; not one thing in all creation was made without him. [4] The Word was the source of life, and this life brought light to mankind. [5] The light shines in the darkness, and the darkness has never put it out.

[6] God sent his messenger, a man named John, [7] who came to tell people about the light, so that all should hear the message and believe. [8] He himself was not the light; he came to tell about the light. [9] This was the real light — the light that comes into the world and shines on all mankind.

[10] The Word was in the world, and though God made the world through him, yet the world did not recognize him. [11] He came to his own country, but his own people did not receive him. [12] Some, however, did receive him and believed in him; so he gave them the right to become God's children. [13] They did not become God's children by natural means, that is, by being born as the children of a human father; God himself was their Father.

[14] The Word became a human being and, full of grace and truth, lived among us. We saw his glory, the glory which he received as the Father's only Son.

[15] John spoke about him. He cried out, 'This is the one I was talking about when I said, "He comes after me, but he is greater than I am, because he existed before I was born."'

[16] Out of the fullness of his grace he has blessed us all, giving us one blessing after another. [17] God gave the Law through Moses, but grace and truth came through Jesus Christ. [18] No one has ever seen God. The only Son, who is the same as God and is at the Father's side, he has made him known.

Some scholars think that John's Gospel originally started with the verses about John the Baptist (vv. 6–9, 15), which seem to break up the rest of this introduction.

As it stands now, John's Gospel does not start with John the Baptist (like Mark's Gospel); it does not even start with the birth of Jesus (like Matthew's and Luke's); it goes right back to the creation of the world. That is where John believed the 'good news' of salvation really started. He believed that there was a sense in which Jesus was there at the very beginning of all things.

The Prologue (John 1:1—18) speaks of Jesus as the Word. A strange title for him, you might think; but it already had a religious meaning in John's day. If you think about it for a moment, you will realise that it was a very good description for John to use of Jesus. John thought that Jesus was the outward appearance on earth of the invisible God; in the same way, a word must first exist unseen in your mind before it is made known to others in its spoken or written form.

The Prologue declares that God the Creator gave people life — not just the physical life which comes to an end when our bodies die — but 'eternal life', the inner life of our spirit which can go on for ever, beyond the grave. This spiritual life can be thought of as a light burning inside us, lighting up our lives. John believed that God came to earth in Jesus to rekindle this light which had gone out in so many people. John describes Jesus as the Light of the World and speaks of his 'glory', or his shining radiance.

1. Copy out the words from verse 1 which you think best put across the idea that Jesus (the Word) was God.
2. Where, in the history of the world, does John begin his Gospel?
3. The 'John' referred to in verses 6–9 is not the writer. Which John is he and what was his task?
4. Christians use the term 'Incarnation' for the belief that God became a man (i.e. Jesus Christ). Read verses 10–14 and pick out the words which best describe the Incarnation. (NB The Incarnation is not the same as 'reincarnation', which is an Indian idea that we are reborn again and again on this earth.)
5. Which verse claims that Jesus was greater than Moses, the great leader and law-giver of the Jews?

Matthew's version

Matthew had evidently been brought up as a strict Jew before turning to Christianity, and he wrote his Gospel for people like himself who were familiar with Judaism. His message to them was that the prophecies about the Messiah in the Jewish Scriptures had come true in Jesus. This was his proof that Jesus really was the Saviour the Jews had all been waiting for.

Matthew starts his Gospel with a family tree. This traces Jesus' descent through Joseph, back to David who was the model for the Messiah, and finally back to Abraham who was the father of the Jews. He then tells the story of Jesus' miraculous birth to Mary, basing it on five Old Testament prophecies, which he

An Ethiopian painting of the wise men.

quotes. In this way Matthew is showing that Jesus and Christianity are continuing what God started in Judaism.

The birth story begins with the couple, Mary and Joseph. They are engaged but not yet properly married. When Mary becomes pregnant, it is Joseph who receives a message from God in his dream telling him that Mary has conceived a son by the Spirit of God and that he is to be called Jesus. Matthew's story progresses by means of a number of messages given in dreams. Those who know the Old Testament might be reminded of an earlier Joseph whose story also revolved around dreams (hence the title of the musical: *Joseph and the Amazing Technicolor Dream-Coat*).

Joseph is a descendant of King David, who lived a thousand years earlier; and Jesus is born in Bethlehem, the town that David himself had come from. Matthew drives home this point because the Messiah was called the Son of David. He was expected to be a New David and it was prophesied that he would come from Bethlehem.

The scene now changes to some wise men, or astrologers, who have travelled from eastern countries because of a star, and have brought gifts to pay their respects to the newborn 'king of the Jews'. This was yet another title for the Messiah because David had been a great king. It was thought that the Messiah would be like him, but an even greater ruler. After David, his son Solomon came to the throne of Israel. Solomon had a reputation for his wisdom and for the splendour of his royal court. There is a famous story in the Bible of the Queen of Sheba bringing exotic gifts to King Solomon. This story has been elaborated in many legends, and a Jewish version has the queen guided to Solomon by a star. Is Matthew thinking of this story when he has the foreign visitors coming with gifts from the east in search of the king of the Jews? If so, Matthew is saying that Jesus is not just a new David, but also a new Solomon.

Egyptian Christians have a legend that the holy family rested in a cave below this church in Cairo.

Naturally enough, the wise men go in search of the new king at the royal palace in the capital city of Jerusalem. Herod the Great was the Jewish king at the time (although subject to the Roman emperor). Herod sends them on to Bethlehem, where the Jews expected the Messiah to be born. He asks them to report back to him if they find the child. The star leads the wise men to Jesus and they present their symbolic gifts of gold, frankincense and myrrh (see section **B**). They are warned in a dream not to return to Herod but to go home by another route.

Joseph also receives warnings in a dream about Herod's wicked plans to kill Jesus. Following God's instructions, Joseph flees the country with his wife and child. They live for a time in Egypt until after Herod's death (in 4 BC). Then they return to Israel and settle in Nazareth, a town up in the north of the country.

When Herod realises that he has been tricked, he sends his soldiers to massacre all children aged two or under in the neighbourhood of Bethlehem. This story of the wicked king and the massacre of the children also has a parallel in the Old Testament. It is like the story of the Pharaoh, the wicked king of Egypt at the time of Moses, who gave orders for all Jewish boys to be killed. God protected Moses who escaped and lived to be the saviour of the Jews. It was he who led them out of slavery in Egypt in the most famous of all the events in Jewish history, the Exodus. Now, Jesus is saved and he too lives to be the Saviour of the Jews. So the story also presents Jesus as the New Moses.

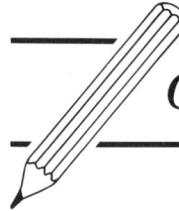

Over to you

1. How does Matthew use Jesus' family tree to show that he was the Messiah?
2. Look up the five prophecies that Matthew quotes in Matthew 1:23; 2:6, 15, 18 and 23. Which parts of the story are they used to illustrate?
3. Why are dreams important in this story?
4. The endings of the following sentences have been muddled up. Write them out with the correct endings.
   a) The wise men went to Herod's palace to find/King Herod.
   b) In the Old Testament, gifts had been brought to the king in Jerusalem by/Joseph.
   c) In the Old Testament, the Egyptian Pharaoh had killed baby Jews, as did/the Queen of Sheba.
   d) The baby Jesus escaped death because God had given a warning in a dream to/the King of the Jews.
5. Because of the similarities with Old Testament stories, Jesus is presented as greater than three very important figures in the Old Testament. Who are they?
6. Consider how Matthew's story of the wise men has grown since it was written down in his Gospel. How many wise men do people say there were? How else are they described? Do you know the names which have been given them (e.g. Balthazar, a black man)?

Art work

On a piece of paper, for display, illustrate just one aspect of the story of Jesus' birth as it appears in Matthew's Gospel.

B 'We Three Kings'

We three kings of Orient are;
Bearing gifts we traverse afar
Field and fountain, moor and mountain,
Following yonder star:
  O star of wonder, star of night,
  Star with royal beauty bright,
  Westward leading, still proceeding,
  Guide us to thy perfect light. (chorus)
Born a king on Bethlehem plain,
Gold I bring, to crown him again —
King for ever, ceasing never,
Over us all to reign: (chorus)
Frankincense to offer have I;
Incense owns a Deity nigh:
Prayer and praising, all men raising,
Worship him, God most high: (chorus)
Myrrh is mine; its bitter perfume
Breathes a life of gathering gloom;
Sorrowing, sighing, bleeding, dying,
Sealed in a stone-cold tomb: (chorus)

Glorious now, behold him arise,
King, and God, and sacrifice!
Heaven sings alleluya,
Alleluya the earth replies: (chorus)

Using this well-known Christmas carol, answer the following questions:

1. *Which of the gifts represents kingship? Copy out a line which expresses this.*
2. *What is burnt in religious services to give off thick clouds of aromatic smoke? Copy out a line about this gift.*
3. *Which gift was used to embalm dead bodies? Copy out a line which makes you think of death.*
4. *Why should things which are normally associated with 'King, and God, and sacrifice' be given to Jesus? What does it tell us about Jesus?*

C Dreams

Where do dreams come from?

'I know it, but I just can't remember it.' Have you ever said that when trying to think of a person's name, or when asked a question in a test? Where has that information gone? It is not in your conscious mind (if it were, you would remember it) but has become unconscious. You may find that later, when you least expect it, the name suddenly comes back to you, rising out of your unconscious into consciousness. Things in the unconscious have not vanished for ever, but are stored away for later use.

We cannot remember everything all the time. Most of our experiences are left in the unconscious, especially those we do not want to remember because they are frightening or disturbing. In dreams, the unconscious mind is at work. Therefore the dream may appear as a distortion or exaggeration of our normal experience.

Interpretation of dreams

Because it comes from a person's unconscious mind, there is no general interpretation of a dream. Each dream is understood only in terms of the person who has had it. Of course, some dream experiences are common, like falling or flying, being chased by something dangerous, running but getting nowhere, becoming very big or very small. This is because people have similar unconscious material in their minds.

Dreams have always been taken seriously by so-called 'primitive' people, and they are now being taken seriously by modern psychologists (doctors of the mind). Dreams unlock hidden parts of the mind and may either remind a person of some event in the past or hint at something that is likely to happen in the future. This is not magic, just the unconscious mind sensing what the future outcome of events might be, and giving warning.

Luke's version

Unlike Matthew who was Jewish, Luke was a Gentile (a non-Jew) and there are many indications that he wrote his Gospel for Gentile Christians. This Gospel also has a family tree for Jesus, but it is very different from Matthew's. In the section from David to Jesus, for example, there are only two names the same. This shows us that the writers were not so much concerned with historical accuracy in saying where Jesus came from, as with the religious question of who he was. Matthew presents him as the Jewish Messiah, but Luke goes back beyond David, and beyond Abraham the first Jew, right back to Adam the first man (Luke 3:38). Luke is saying that the birth of Jesus is important for all humanity, not just for the Jews. Similarly, Luke puts the birth of Jesus in a world-wide setting, telling us the names of the Roman rulers at the time and giving the Roman census as the reason for Joseph and Mary being in Bethlehem, where Jesus was born.

Despite Luke's interest in Gentiles, we still find a strong Jewish background to his Christmas story. It could hardly be otherwise for Jesus was a Jew, Christianity grew out of Judaism and Jesus was believed to be the Christ, i.e. the Messiah, whom the Jews were expecting.

In this Gospel women play quite an important part, and it is Mary herself who is visited by the angel Gabriel to explain to her about her pregnancy:

Caves like this, in the hillsides around Bethlehem, were used by shepherds and farmers to shelter their animals. The stable in Luke's story could well have been a cave.

The market in the town of Bethlehem today.

The angel said to her, 'Don't be afraid, Mary; God has been gracious to you. You will become pregnant and give birth to a son, and you will name him Jesus. He will be great and will be called the Son of the Most High God. The Lord God will make him a king, as his ancestor David was, and he will be the king of the descendants of Jacob for ever; his kingdom will never end!' (Luke 1:30–3)

This passage is full of references to the Messiah, although it never actually uses that name. *Jesus*, the Greek version of Joshua, meant 'Saviour'. *Son of the Most High God* referred to the Messiah, the Son of God. It speaks of his ancestor *David* because another title for the Messiah was 'Son of David'. The *descendants of Jacob* were the Jews and the Messiah was to be 'King of the Jews'.

Another Jewish element in Luke's Christmas story is the use of hymns of praise, just like those in the Old Testament book of Psalms, which Jews have always used in their worship. The song of Mary, known to the Church as the Magnificat (see section **D**), expresses Mary's joy that at last God is keeping his promise to save his people, and that *she* has been chosen to be part of God's saving act.

The central part of Luke's Christmas story is the well-known episode when Mary and Joseph have to travel to be registered from their home town of Nazareth all the way south to Bethlehem where Joseph's family had come from (see map on page 6). At best it was a six days' journey on foot or donkey, but now it was particularly difficult, for Mary was heavily pregnant.

When they arrived in Bethlehem, the little town was bursting at the seams, and they could find nowhere to stay apart from a stable. It was probably one of the caves which shepherds and farmers still use in this area. Mary gave birth to her son there in the stable and used the cattle's feeding-trough for a cot.

Out on the hills, we are told that shepherds were looking after their flocks when God sent them the good news of the birth of the Messiah:

An angel of the Lord appeared to them, and the glory of the Lord shone over them. They were terribly afraid, but the angel said to them, 'Don't be afraid! I am here with good news for you, which will bring great joy to all the people. This very day in David's town your Saviour was born — Christ the Lord!' (Luke 2:9–11)

The shepherds went to Bethlehem and found everything as the angel had said.

What should strike you, when reading this story after Matthew's, is the difference in atmosphere between the two. We do not have a baby being worshipped and offered exotic gifts by astrologers from the east. Instead, we have ordinary shepherds, two weary northerners taking shelter in a stable far from home, and a newborn baby wrapped up against the cold in a makeshift bed. There is no worldly splendour in Luke's account. This birth story reflects the way Jesus was to live later on as he travelled about Palestine with 'nowhere to lie down and rest' (Luke 9:58), bringing the 'good news' of salvation to the poor.

Over to you

1. For whom was Luke's Gospel written?
2. Why does Luke's version of Jesus' family tree go back to Adam?
3. What did the name 'Jesus' mean?
4. In the message of the angel to the shepherds, why is it important that Jesus is born 'in David's town'?
5. List as many titles for the Messiah as you can find.
6. Finish the following sentence in at least two different ways, putting your most important answer first: *Luke's Christmas story teaches us that Jesus was born to* _____

D The Magnificat

The Song of Mary in Luke's Gospel (1:46—55) is called the Magnificat by the Church (because it is the first word of this psalm in the Latin version).

Mary said,
'My heart praises the Lord;
my soul is glad because of God my Saviour,
for he has remembered me, his lowly servant!
From now on all people will call me happy,
because of the great things the Mighty God
    has done for me.
His name is holy;
from one generation to another
he shows mercy to those who honour him.
He has stretched out his mighty arm
and scattered the proud with all their plans.
He has brought down mighty kings from their
    thrones,
and lifted up the lowly.
He has filled the hungry with good things,
and sent the rich away with empty hands.
He has kept the promise he made to our
    ancestors,
and has come to the help of his servant Israel.
He has remembered to show mercy to Abraham
and to all his descendants for ever!'

1. *If you had to put this poem to music, what type of music would you choose and what feeling would you want to express?*
2. *Look up a similar psalm in the Old Testament, spoken by Hannah when God answered her prayers for a child: I Samuel 2:1–10. Copy out any lines which are very similar to the Magnificat.*
3. *'He has filled the hungry with good things, and sent the rich away with empty hands' is an important theme in Luke's Gospel. Write down what is said about the hungry and the rich in Luke 6:20–6.*
4. *The last four lines of the Magnificat refer to God's promise to the descendants of Abraham:*
   a) *Who are they? (If necessary, look up 'Abraham' in the Word list.)*
   b) *What did God promise them?*
   c) *How did Mary help God to keep his promise?*
5. *Try to sum up, in one sentence, what the Magnificat is saying.*

E The animals in the Christmas story

Do you think there were animals in the stable where Jesus was born, and did the shepherds bring an offering of a lamb? You can check the answer in Luke 2:7 and 15—20. The tradition that there was an ox and ass in the stable, worshipping the baby Jesus, comes from Isaiah 1:3:

The ox knows it owner,
  and the ass its master's crib. (*RSV*)

The following modern poem recalls an old legend, still told by country people, about animals kneeling at midnight on Christmas Eve.

It is traditional to make models of the nativity scene. These are called cribs, and can be seen in churches and other places at Christmas time. Which Gospel story is modelled here? (Is it from Matthew's or Luke's Gospel?)

The Oxen

Christmas Eve, and twelve of the clock.
  'Now they are all on their knees,'
An elder said as we sat in a flock
  By the embers in hearthside ease.

We pictured the meek mild creatures where
  They dwelt in their strawy pen,
Nor did it occur to one of us there
  To doubt they were kneeling then.

So fair a fancy few would weave
  In these years! Yet, I feel,
If someone said on Christmas Eve,
  'Come; see the oxen kneel

'In the lonely barton by yonder coomb
  Our childhood used to know,'
I should go with him in the gloom,
  Hoping it might be so.

Thomas Hardy

81

Jesus' childhood

There were three ceremonies which followed Jesus' birth, to fulfil the Jewish Law. The first was his circumcision and naming on the eighth day, as a sign that he was a Jew. For forty days after giving birth to a son, the mother was considered to be ritually unclean. So it was forty days before Mary could go up to the Temple at Jerusalem and offer sacrifices for her cleansing. We are told that Mary offered two birds, since she obviously could not afford the alternative of a lamb and a bird. She and Joseph also perform-

Jewish baby boys are still circumcised at eight days old, as Jesus was. The foreskin is removed. This is a sign of being Jewish and having a special relationship with God.

ed the third ceremony there. Jews consider that a first-born son belongs to God and has to be bought back from him with a small offering of five shekels. What is interesting in Luke's account is that Mary does not buy Jesus back at all, but instead she offers him to God. Maybe Luke was just confused over these Jewish rituals, or is he making the point that Jesus was to live as a servant of God?

The setting of part of the story in the Temple at Jerusalem is important, for this was where the Jews expected the Messiah to appear. Jerusalem was also important to Luke because it was from here that the Good News was taken to the rest of the (Gentile) world. Luke's attitude to Jesus is summed up perfectly in the

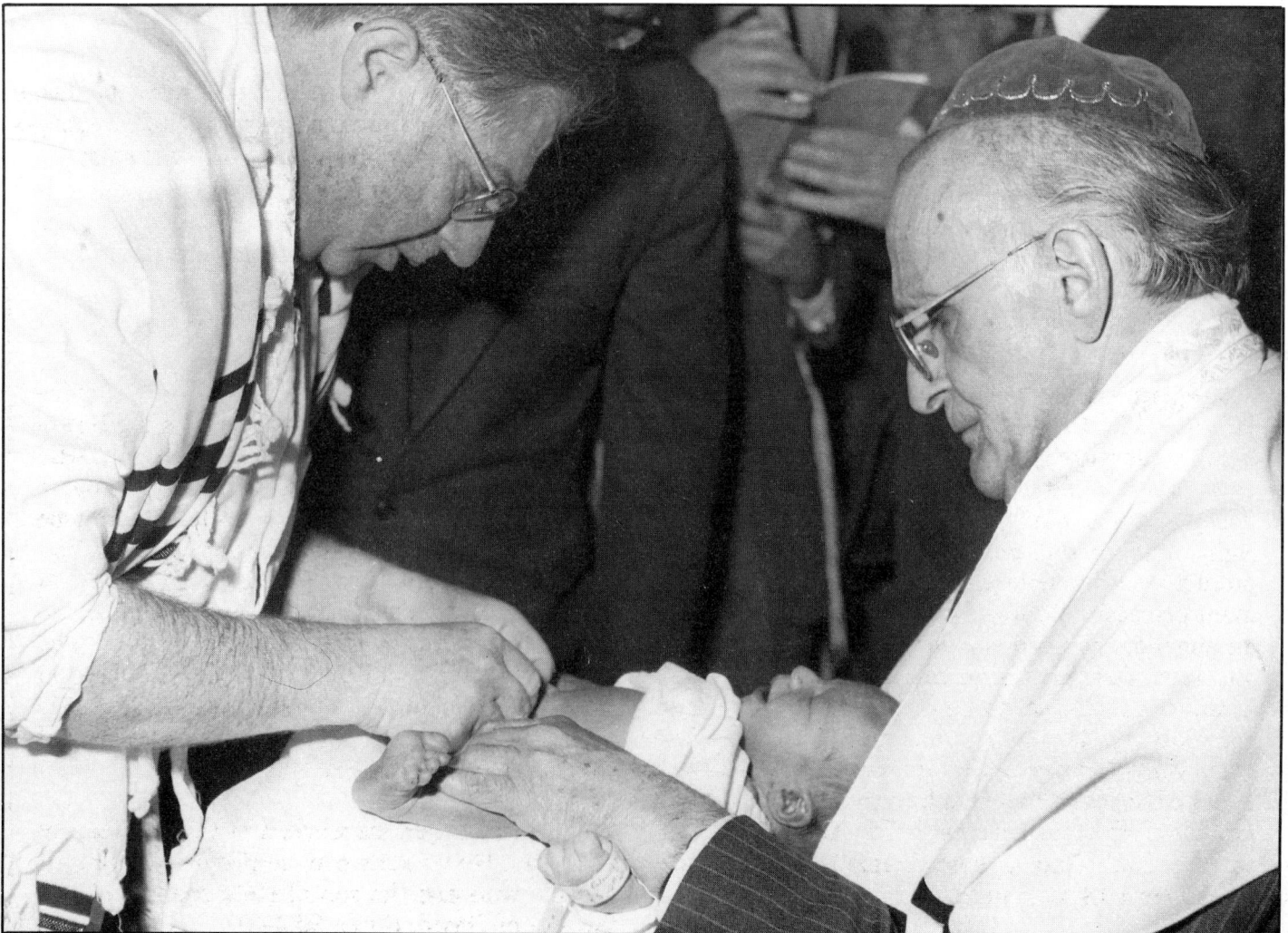

words of Simeon, a devout old man who came up to them in the Temple. He declared that the baby Jesus was:

'A light to reveal your [God's] will to the Gentiles
and bring glory to your people Israel.' (Luke 2:32)

The only story of Jesus' childhood in the Bible follows on from Luke's birth story. Jesus was now twelve years old and approaching the age of maturity in Judaism. He went with his parents on their annual visit to Jerusalem for the Passover festival. He got so involved with the religious debates in the Temple that he stayed behind there, even after his parents had packed up and left for home. At first Mary and Joseph assumed that he was with their party from Nazareth, but when he had not shown up by the end of the day they turned back. Imagine their relief when, after three days, they found him safe and sound in the Temple. He was discussing religion with the Jewish teachers and surprising everyone with his intelligence. The punch line of the story comes when Mary asked Jesus what he thought he was up to, treating his parents like that, and Jesus replied:

'Didn't you know that I had to be in my Father's house?' (Luke 2:49)

Luke is showing us that, as Jesus grew up, he was aware of his special relationship with God and was just waiting for the sign to begin his ministry.

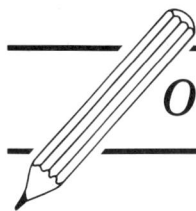

Over to you

1. Which three rituals were performed at the birth of a first boy?
2. Act out the story of Jesus' childhood. You may want to read it first in Luke 2:41–52.
3. Many years later Jesus received the sign to begin his ministry. What was it? (See page 25.)

Art work

Choose just one aspect from the story of Jesus' birth or childhood as it appears in Luke's Gospel. Illustrate this on a piece of paper for display.

F The Virgin Birth

This was how the birth of Jesus Christ took place. His mother Mary was engaged to Joseph, but before they were married, she found out that she was going to have a baby by the Holy Spirit. Joseph was a man who always did what was right, but he did not want to disgrace Mary publicly; so he made plans to break the engagement privately. While he was thinking about this, an angel of the Lord appeared to him in a dream and said, 'Joseph, descendant of David, do not be afraid to take Mary to be your wife. For it is by the Holy Spirit that she has conceived. . . . So when Joseph woke up, he married Mary, as the angel of the Lord had told him to do. But he had no sexual relations with her before she gave birth to her son. And Joseph named him Jesus. (Matthew 1:18–20 and 24–5)

God sent the angel Gabriel to a town in Galilee named Nazareth. He had a message for a girl promised in marriage to a man named Joseph, who was a descendant of King David. The girl's name was Mary . . . The angel said to her, 'Don't be afraid, Mary; God has been gracious to you. You will become pregnant and give birth to a son, and you will name him Jesus . . .' Mary said to the angel, 'I am a virgin. How, then, can this be?' The angel answered, 'The Holy Spirit will come on you, and God's power will rest upon you. For this reason the holy child will be called the Son of God.' (Luke 1:26–7, 30–1 and 34–5)

When Jesus began his work, he was about thirty years old. He was the son, so people thought, of Joseph, who was the son of Heli, the son of . . . the son of David. (Luke 3:23–31)

This is an icon of Mary and Jesus from the Russian Orthodox Church. Icons are special holy paintings used by Christians in worship. What do you think a worshipper might think when looking at this holy picture?

Christians are divided over whether or not to take the virgin birth of Jesus as historical fact. Mary, 'the Mother of God', plays a very important part in the Orthodox and Roman Catholic Churches, and is held by them to have really been a virgin. The Roman Catholic Church goes so far as to teach the perpetual virginity of Mary, i.e. that she never had sexual intercourse, even after Jesus was born. If so, Jesus' brothers and sisters, mentioned in Mark 6:3, may have been older half-brothers and sisters, from a previous marriage of Joseph's. (Only Mary is mentioned in the Gospels during the time of Jesus' ministry, which led to the idea that Joseph was much older than Mary when they married and that he was dead by this time.) Christians who accept the virgin birth of Jesus see this to be yet another miracle connected with Jesus and brought about by the power of God. If Mary was a virgin when she gave birth to Jesus, then she had not conceived him in the usual way, through sexual intercourse (and there were no test-tube babies in those days).

Other Christians find this hard to accept. This is not just because it goes against the laws of nature, which were created by God. It is mainly because, with our present knowledge of human conception (and how babies take half their genes from their mother and the other half from their father), it would mean that we cannot really say that Jesus was fully human — which is a basic Christian belief.

If we look again at the Gospel stories, we see that on the one hand they portray Jesus' miraculous birth to the virgin Mary; but on the other hand they claim Jesus' important descent back to King David, through Joseph. Now, if these were historical documents, we should be right in saying that they cannot have it both ways. But Matthew and Luke did not seem to worry about this, and this is one of the clues that we are not to take these stories as just history or biology. We should rather be looking for the religious message that the stories convey. The Virgin Birth story stated two things very clearly to the early Christians. First, that God was involved in Jesus' birth and that he was the 'Son of God' — the Messiah. Second, that Jesus was also a real human being who had developed in the usual way, inside a woman's womb. The concern to say that Jesus was descended from David was a way of saying that he was the 'Son of David' — the Messiah.

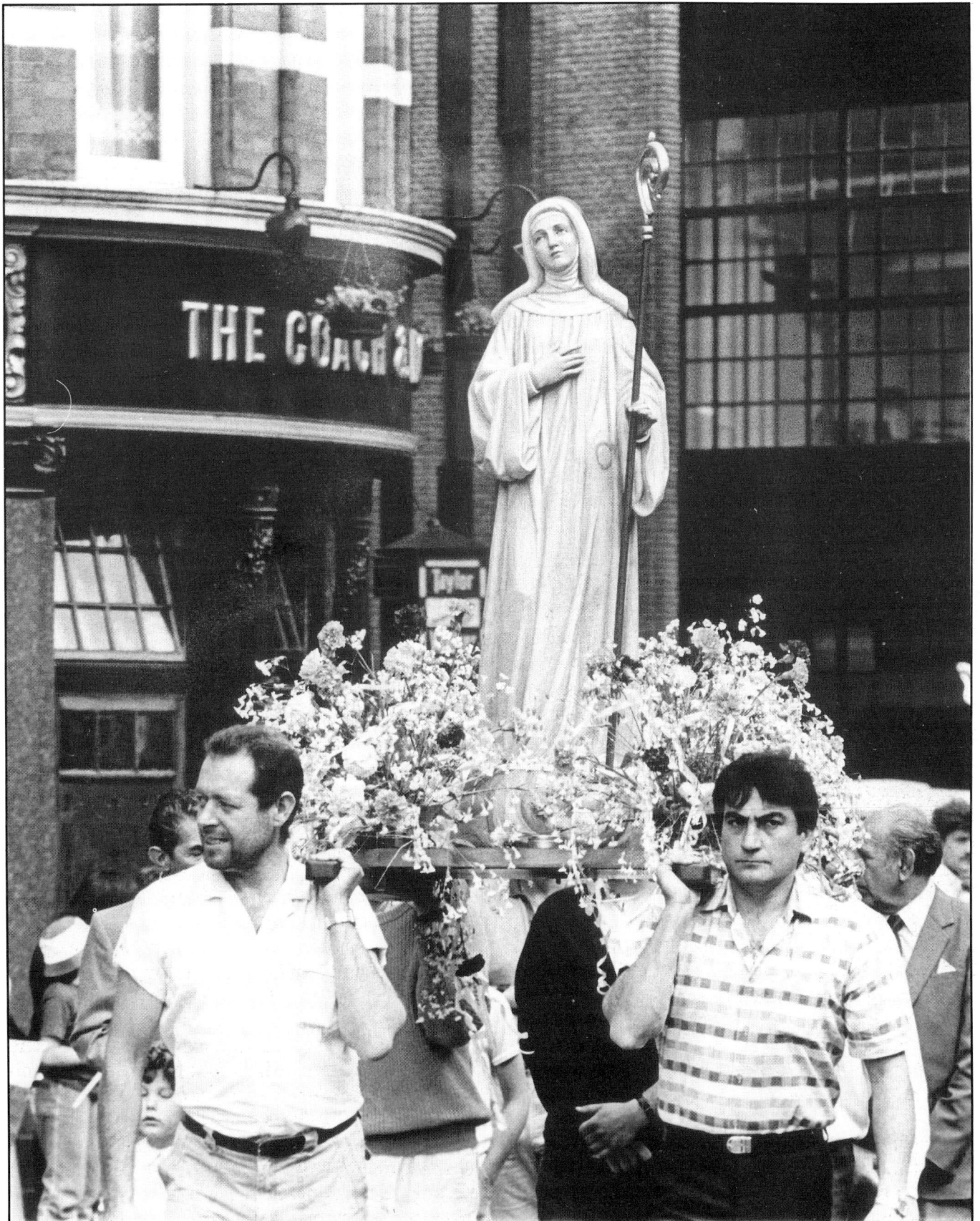

In Roman Catholic communities, statues of the Virgin Mary are carried in procession through the streets at special festivals. This procession is in Clerkenwell, London.

Introduction

This book began with an account of the Resurrection. The Resurrection convinced Jesus' earliest followers that he had conquered death. Now they were sure that he was the Messiah.

The books which were called Gospels set down things which Jesus was reported to have said and done. They were written to proclaim the belief that Jesus was the Messiah and to win others to this faith. Mark's Gospel opens with the words:

This is the Good News about Jesus Christ, the Son of God.

The other Gospels have fuller introductions,

'Jesus said "Go, then, to all peoples everywhere and make them my disciples."' The Christian Gospel is now preached throughout the world. Where do you think this photograph was taken?

but the birth stories and John's Prologue are different ways of explaining and emphasising the belief which is summed up by Mark in this one verse.

The endings of the Gospels are also similar in what they have to say. They all record the final conflict, the Cross and the Resurrection, but they do not stop here. They point the reader onwards to the continuation of Jesus' work in the Church. Matthew's Gospel finishes with a final resurrection appearance of Jesus to his disciples, when he gives them this last command:

'Go, then, to all peoples everywhere and make them my disciples: baptize them in the name of the Father, the Son, and the Holy Spirit, and teach them to obey everything I have commanded you. And I will be with you always, to the end of the age.' (Matthew 28:19–20)

At the end of Luke's Gospel, Jesus tells his disciples that, in the Messiah's name, 'the message about repentance and the forgiveness of sins must be preached to all nations' (Luke 24:47). He assures them that God will give them the power to do this. There then follows the scene where Jesus left his disciples 'and was taken up into heaven' (see section A).

John's Gospel may well have finished originally at chapter 20. This looks forward to the time when people would believe in Jesus even when they had not seen him on earth. The final chapter also speaks of future Christian believers. There is a resurrection story of a miraculous catch of fish. We are told that 153 big fish filled the net but did not break it. Many Christian readers have understood this to represent the Church. The Church is like a net which draws together many different types of people and joins them together in following Jesus Christ.

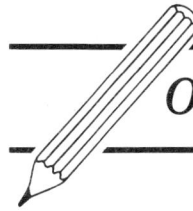

Over to you

1. Which word, from the first verse of Mark's Gospel, is the Greek form of 'Messiah'?
2. The ending of Mark's Gospel is not mentioned above. This is because we cannot be sure how it originally finished. There have been a variety of later endings added to the Gospel. Look up Mark 16 in a modern version of the Bible and copy out the final verse that remains of the original ending.
3. Read Acts 2:1–3. This is the story of how God's power, the Holy Spirit, came to the disciples. Wind and fire are used here as symbols of God's power. Give some examples of how both wind and fire can be very powerful. Illustrate your answers if you wish.

A The Ascension

These stories, by the same writer, express the Christian belief that Jesus' rightful place, as the Messiah, was with God in glory. Also, the second account expresses the belief that Christ will one day return in glory to judge the world and complete the Kingdom of God.

Then he led them out of the city as far as Bethany, where he raised his hands and blessed them. As he was blessing them, he departed from them and was taken up into heaven. They worshipped him and went back into Jerusalem, filled with great joy, and spent all their time in the Temple giving thanks to God. (Luke 24:50–3)

He was taken up to heaven as they watched him, and a cloud hid him from their sight. They still had their eyes fixed on the sky as he went away, when two men dressed in white suddenly stood beside them and said, 'Galileans, why are you standing there looking up at the sky? This Jesus, who was taken from you into heaven, will come back in the same way that you saw him go to heaven.' (Acts 1:9–11)

Christian teaching and beliefs

After the resurrection appearances had stopped, the disciples *did* find the power to carry on Jesus' work. We are told in The Acts of the Apostles that the Holy Spirit came upon them. Some Christians believe that this is the Spirit of Christ, continuing to live in the world through his followers.

This shows a Gospel procession in a Roman Catholic church. The man in front is swinging a special container of incense, which burns with smoke and a sweet smell. The priest carries the service book with the Gospel readings in it to the place where it is read. He is accompanied by candle bearers. Why do you think they take so much trouble over this?

So the Gospel story of Jesus continues in the Church that the disciples started. The Good News soon spread beyond the Jews to the Gentiles and Christianity became a world religion. People who had never known Jesus as a man in Palestine came to put their trust in him. Today, Christianity is claimed to be the largest of all the religions in the world.

As Christianity developed, people wanted to understand more about the meaning of Jesus Christ. How was he God's Son? Was he both human and divine? How does Jesus exist today? What is meant by his Second Coming? The more you think about the Gospel story, the more questions there are to ask about Jesus.

The Church goes on asking these questions. It believes that God has given us our minds and that we should use them to try to understand more about him. But it says that reason alone is not enough. There is also revelation, i.e. God has made himself known to his people. Christians believe that God has revealed himself most of all in the person of Jesus — known to us through the Gospels.

Down the ages, Christians have struggled with all these questions about Jesus and often they have come to different conclusions. But they have always based their arguments on passages from the Gospels, and started from the basic belief that Jesus was the Messiah.

Over to you

1. How did some Christians believe that Jesus had kept his promise (in Matthew 28:20) that he would be with them always, to the end of the age?
2. How many are said to have joined the disciples after Peter's first sermon in Jerusalem (see Acts 2:41)?

Christian worship

The Gospel story of 2,000 years ago is still read by Christians today in their services. These were based on the Jewish synagogue services, where the most important part was the reading from the Scriptures. The Jewish Scriptures have passed into Christianity as the Old Testament. The New Testament was added to it, to form the Christian Bible. The reading of passages from this Bible, and explaining them in sermons, has always been an important part of Church services. In some Churches, the Gospel reading is the most important of all. In these Churches there is a procession, carrying the Gospels, or the whole Bible, to where the priest is to read it, and everyone stands for this. In other Churches, the preaching of the Gospel is considered most important. The sermon emphasises the Good News that Jesus came as the Messiah, and people are encouraged to accept him as their saviour.

It is interesting to see that the Gospels are used in Church services in a piecemeal way. The readings from the Gospels each Sunday do not usually work through each Gospel in turn from beginning to end. The Gospels are not treated as biographies which have to be read through in order. Instead, passages are selected to fit in with festivals of the Church. Sermons are preached on individual passages, or quotations are drawn from all over the Gospels on a particular theme.

This is also the way the Gospel stories were originally used, before they were written down. A story might have been used by an early Christian to teach a particular point about Jesus. Some of Jesus' sayings on the same theme were remembered together. In this way, separate units of material were passed down (apart from the stories of Jesus' death and resurrection, which follow an obvious progression from one event to the next). It was up to the Gospel writers to arrange these separate stories as they saw fit, using just a few basic landmarks like his birth at the beginning and his death at the end. However well arranged the Gospels are, the separate units in them remain clear. You can open a Gospel almost anywhere, start reading at a new paragraph, and find that it makes sense. This would not be true of most other types of books.

A group of Christians in Nigeria are discussing the meaning of a Bible passage.

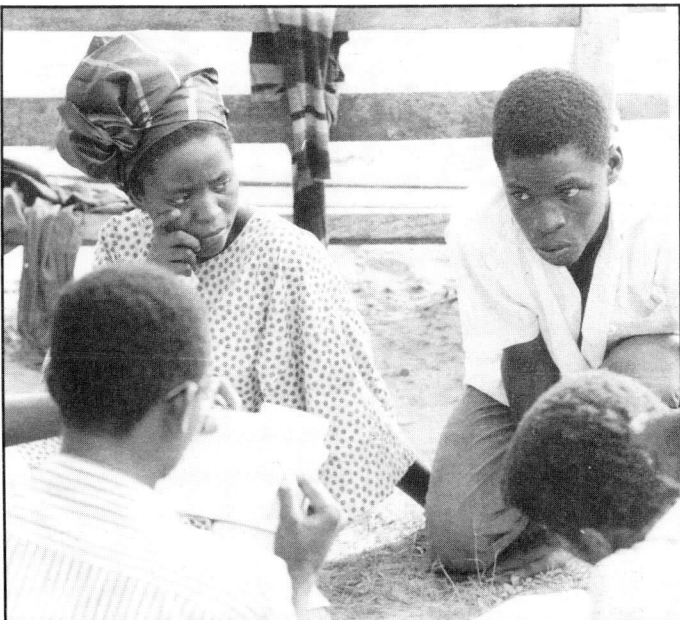

Over to you

1. a) What are the two parts of the Christian Bible?
   b) In which part are the Gospels?
2. Which Gospel stories would you expect to be read in Church on
   a) Christmas Day, and
   b) Easter Sunday?
   (Look up these festivals in the Word list if you need to.)
3. Test for yourself the theory that the Gospels are made up of separate stories. Open a Gospel somewhere in the middle and see if you can find a complete story. (Some modern versions of the Bible give helpful sub-headings.) Write down what the story is about, with its reference.

B The creeds

As time went on, the Gospel story was summed up in the creeds of the Church (from the Latin word *credo* — 'I believe'). These statements of belief were written to define the Christian faith and to preserve it from being changed by people who interpreted the Gospel material in different ways. The creeds were shorthand forms of the Gospel story.

This is the main section, the part about Jesus, from the Nicene Creed (which dates from the late fourth, or fifth century). All these beliefs about Jesus can be supported by reference to the Gospels.

We believe in one Lord, Jesus Christ,
the only Son of God,
eternally begotten of the Father,
God from God, Light from Light,
true God from true God,
begotten, not made,
of one Being with the Father.
Through him all things were made.
For us men and for our salvation
he came down from heaven;
by the power of the Holy Spirit
he became incarnate of the Virgin Mary,
    and was made man.
For our sake he was crucified under
    Pontius Pilate;
he suffered death and was buried.
On the third day he rose again
in accordance with the Scriptures;

he ascended into heaven
and is seated at the right hand of the Father.
He will come again in glory
to judge the living and the dead,
and his kingdom will have no end.

The first section here is similar to the opening of John's Gospel and emphasises the godliness of Jesus Christ. The second section speaks of the Incarnation — that God became man in Jesus. The third section speaks of Jesus' death and resurrection, and also the belief that he reigns in glory with God now. The last section here speaks of the Second Coming of Christ to earth, to reign over his Kingdom in glory.

1. *Read the first five verses of John's Gospel (page 74) and make a note of the similarities with the first section that is quoted here from the Nicene Creed.*
2. *Which Gospels record stories of the virgin birth of Jesus?*
3. *Which Gospel writer tells us that Jesus went up into heaven (see section A)?*
4. *What is meant by the imagery of Jesus being seated 'at the right hand of the Father'? Consider what we mean by a 'right-hand man'.*
5. *What did Christians believe Jesus would do when he returned to earth? What parable contains this idea (see page 41)?*

Christian Church •
† Church and main centre of Christianity

The first followers of Jesus spread Christianity from Jerusalem as far as Rome, the capital city of the Roman Empire. By the 4th century it was well established throughout the Mediterranean lands, with its fifth main centre at Constantinople (shown in brackets on the map). As more of the world was discovered, so Christianity spread even further, to become the biggest of the world religions. It is now to be found on all parts of the globe.

Christian living

Christians have often responded to the problems of inner-city life. This boy might be enjoying himself, but what are the dangers of playing in a place like this? Can you name any famous Christians who have worked to help those suffering in the inner cities? (Clues: one man started a famous children's home which took children off the streets of London; one woman works in Calcutta, in India.)

Christians believe that Jesus came to set an example of how God wants people to live. So, once more, Christians turn back to the Gospels for their information about how Jesus himself lived and what he taught others to do. It is not always easy for a Christian to know what is the right thing to do. Some of our modern problems, like abortion, did not seem to be an issue for people of Jesus' day. Nevertheless, the Church has always looked first at suitable examples from the Gospels in the belief that the Holy Spirit will guide Christians in their understanding, so that they know what is right.

In following Christ, sincere Christians try to live out the Gospel story in their own lives, continuing the work of Jesus on earth. This is expressed in a famous Christian prayer by St Teresa. She was a nun who lived in the sixteenth century, and she is called a 'saint' because it is thought that she was particularly holy.

Christ has no body now on earth but yours,
No hands but yours,
No feet but yours.
Yours are the eyes through which is to look out
  Christ's compassion on the world.
Yours are the feet with which he is to go about
  doing good.
Yours are the hands with which he is to bless
  men now. Amen.

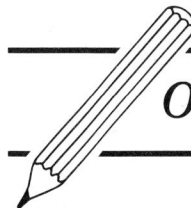

Over to you

1. Which modern problems would you not expect to find anything about in the Gospels?
2. Try to make up your own poem, like the one above but with different examples. It should put across the idea that Christ's work must be done in the world today by his followers.

C 'Living Lord'

This modern Christian hymn is called 'Living Lord'. It expresses the Christian belief that Jesus lives today. This does not mean that he is walking about somewhere, as he once did in Palestine. Christians mean that Jesus lives on in spirit. They claim that they can each know him personally; that he inspires their thoughts; and that he gives them his power to carry on his work on earth.

Lord Jesus Christ,
you have come to us,
you are one with us,
  Mary's Son.
Cleansing our souls from all their sin,
pouring your love and goodness in;
Jesus, our love for you we sing,
  Living Lord.

Lord Jesus Christ,
I would come to you,
live my life for you,
  Son of God.
All your commands I know are true,
your many gifts will make me new,
into my life your power breaks through,
  Living Lord.

1. *What does it mean if you recognise someone as your Lord?*
2. *What does this hymn claim that Jesus does for Christians, so proving that he is alive today in their lives?*
3. *How can someone live his or her life for Jesus?*

Christians in Nigeria are listening to a new translation of the Bible into their language, to check that it sounds right.

Conclusion

This book has explained that the Gospel story of Jesus grew out of the belief in Jesus' resurrection. On this basis, each Gospel writer in his own way proclaimed the 'good news' that Jesus was the Christ. Two thousand years later, we still have the Gospels. Unlike some ancient writings, they are not just kept in museums or libraries, or just studied for examinations. Millions of people all over the world have copies of the Gospels, translated from the ancient Greek into their own languages. The Gospel story of Jesus continues to be the 'good news' of Christians today. It is a living story: alive in the Church's teachings and worship, and still lived out by the followers of Jesus Christ.

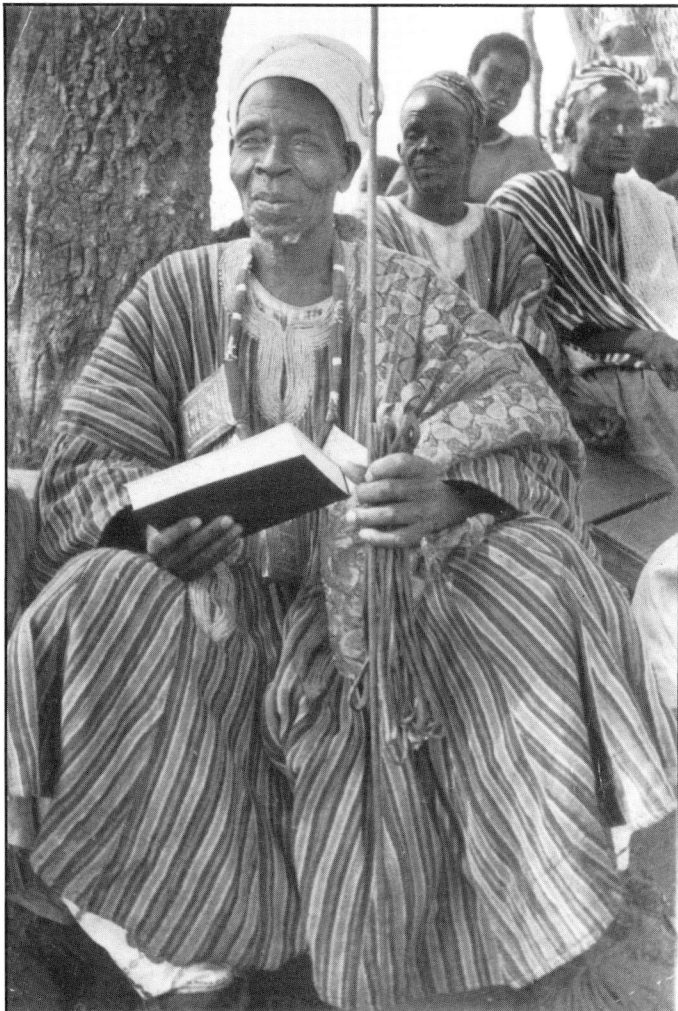

(above) Today the 'good news' about Jesus is translated into many languages.

(left) A Tampulma chief in Ghana holds a copy of the Tampulma New Testament, translated by members of the Wycliffe Bible Translators from Britain. Choose one word to describe how you think he feels.

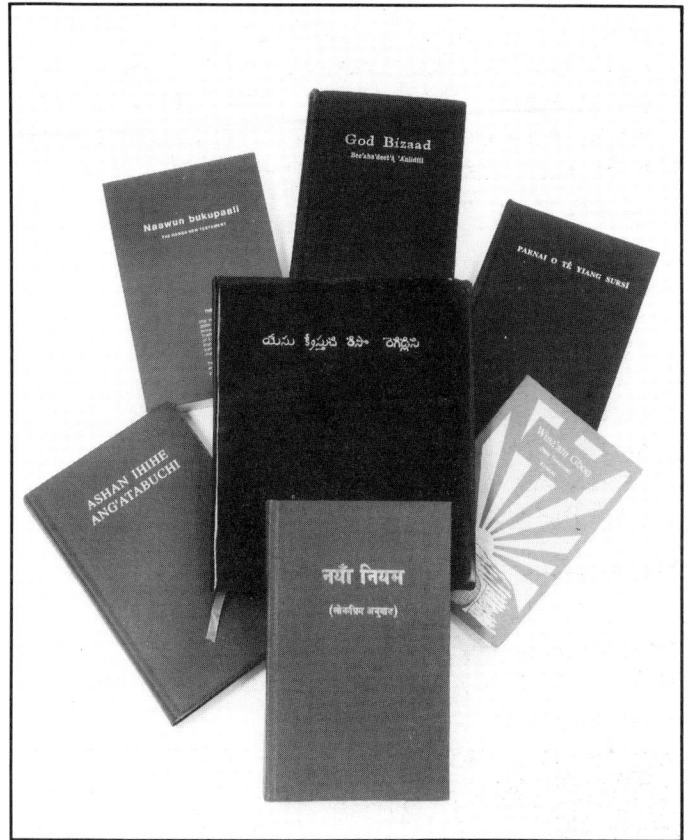

93

Word list

Abraham — the father, or earliest ancestor, of the Jews

angel — a 'messenger' and servant of God

apostle — title used in the Gospels for the twelve disciples who were 'sent forth' to do Jesus' work

ascension — going up (of Jesus into heaven)

baptism — a religious ceremony in which someone is immersed in water or splashed with it, as a sign of inner purity and/or becoming a member of that religion (see page 23)

baptize — to administer baptism to somebody

blasphemy — speaking against God

Christ — the Greek for Messiah, the 'anointed one', the saviour awaited by the Jews

Christian — (noun) a follower of Jesus Christ, i.e. someone who believes that Jesus is the Messiah; (adjective) of Christianity

Christianity — the religion of the followers of Jesus Christ

Christmas — the Church festival which celebrates the birth of Jesus Christ

Church — the congregation of Christian people; also used of the building in which Christians meet to worship

crucifixion — a method of execution, used a great deal by the Romans; the victim was hung on a wooden cross until he died (see page 10)

crucify — to kill by crucifixion

demon — a harmful, evil spirit; a messenger and servant of the Devil

demon-possession — to be taken over by one or more demons; some illnesses, particularly mental ones, were thought to be caused by demons living inside people

disciple — a 'learner', a follower of a teacher; used especially of the twelve disciples of Jesus, who were also called apostles

divine — godly, of God

Easter — the Church festival which celebrates the death of Jesus (on Good Friday) and his resurrection (on Easter Sunday)

exorcism — the casting out of evil spirits (see page 56)

Gentile — someone who is not Jewish

gospel — 'good news' that Jesus is the Messiah; it was first preached and then written down in books called Gospels

Holy Communion — a Church service in which bread and wine are used as symbols of Jesus' body and blood; it can also be called the Eucharist and Mass (see pages 57–9)

Judaism — the religion of the Jews (see page 43)

Kingdom of God/Heaven — the reign of God and time of salvation

martyr — a 'witness' who dies for his/her faith

material — (as opposed to **spiritual**) to do with matter, physical things

Messiah — the 'anointed one', the saviour awaited by the Jews (see page 26)

Messianic — of the Messiah

miracle — a wonderful, supernatural event; Jesus' miracles were also spoken of as signs or acts of power

monastery — the place where monks live

monastic	to do with monks
monk	someone who wants to be 'alone' to pray, and dedicates his life to God
parable	a story which puts across its meaning by drawing a comparison with some everyday event
Passover	an annual Jewish festival which commemorates the Exodus, the escape of the Jews from Egypt under Moses (see pages 70–1)
Pharisee	a member of a religious party of 'separated ones' who kept strictly to the Jewish laws
pilgrim	a person who visits a religious place as an act of worship
prophecy	the message a prophet proclaimed
prophet	'one who proclaims' God's messages, a spokesman/woman for God, and therefore a religious teacher
rabbi	'my teacher'; title used for a Jewish religious teacher
repent	to 'turn around'; to be sorry for your sins and change your ways
repentance	the process of repenting, being sorry for what you have done
resurrection	the raising to life from death
righteous	to do with what is good and right
ritual	a ceremony
Sabbath	the Jewish holy day, the day of rest when they 'cease' from work (see page 61)
sacrifice	an offering, especially something precious given up to God in worship
Sadducee	a member of the conservative religious party in Judaism, associated with the Temple; they were the nobility and mostly priests
salvation	being saved; used in a religious sense to mean that a person gains eternal life
Satan	the Devil, the supreme power of evil
sign	something which points beyond itself to something else; Jesus' miracles were called 'signs' in John's Gospel because they indicated that he was the Messiah
sin	wrong-doing against God
spiritual	(as opposed to **material**) to do with spirit rather than matter
symbol	something which represents something else
synagogue	a 'meeting' of Jews; the place where they assemble for worship (see page 62)
temptation	an urge to do wrong
unclean	not fit to worship God or be used in his worship; not permitted by the Law of Judaism
Zealot	a Jewish nationalist who fought to free Israel from Roman rule

Index